LIVING THE MAGICAL LIFE

ALSO BY SUZI GABLIK

Magritte

Has Modernism Failed?

The Reenchantment of Art

Conversations Before the End of Time

Living the Magical Life

An Oracular Adventure

Suzi Gablik

Phanes Press

© 2002 by Suzi Gablik
All rights reserved. No part of this publication may be reproduced or transmitted in any form or by any means, electronic or mechanical, including photocopying, recording, or by any information storage and retrieval system, with the exception of short excerpts used in reviews, without permission in writing from the publisher.

PHANES PRESS, INC.
PO Box 6114
Grand Rapids, MI 49516
www.phanes.com

9 8 7 6 5 4 3 2 1
Printed in the United States of America
∞ This edition is printed on acid-free paper
that meets the American National Standards Institute Z39.48 Standard.

Library of Congress Cataloging-in-Publication Data
Gablik, Suzi.
Living the magical life : an oracular adventure / Suzi Gablik.
p. cm.
ISBN 1-890482-86-2 (alk. paper)
1. Gablik, Suzi. 2. Spiritual biography. I. Title
BL73.G32 A3 2002
291.4'092—dc21
[B]
2002073252

Chapters

One	9
Two	17
Three	23
Four	31
Five	39
Six	47
Seven	53
Eight	59
Nine	65
Ten	71
Eleven	75
Twelve	83
Thirteen	89
Fourteen	97
Fifteen	103
Sixteen	109
Seventeen	115
Eighteen	123
Nineteen	129
Twenty	135
Twenty-one	143

Twenty-two	149
Twenty-three	159
Twenty-four	165
Twenty-five	173
Twenty-six	181
Twenty-seven	187
Twenty-eight	193
Twenty-nine	199
Epilogue	205

You may be hearing a call to change . . . Your life is going to change. And when it does you will probably never be able to return to your old ways, your old life. And it's possible your friends won't recognize you as the same person they used to know.

—Carlos Warter

Someone who has tasted the air inside the Rose,
do you think he'd go back
to drinking wine in the steambath?

—Jelaluddin Rumi

The secret of a soul-based life is to allow someone or something other than the usual self to be in charge.

—Thomas Moore

One

I LIKE TO SIT, in the evening, at my Black Madonna altar, its candles burning as if I were in Chartres or Notre-Dame or Saint-Michel. As the incense slowly turns to ash, its fragrance scents the whole house. I like to sit before the Black Madonna as a way of finding out what the gods want, even though I know that finding out what the gods want is held to be of little value in our society and has been discontinued as a practice. Inviting the gods in, I often wonder whether this "magical" dimension of life eludes us only because we have disavowed it. No longer the critic who stands back to analyze an issue, and wearing a different cultural lens, I can now step directly into the drama myself, to get at something "utterly heartbroken," as Annie Dillard puts it in one of her poems: "colors, which have no name, but are the real foundation of everything."

When I moved to Virginia in 1991 after living in London for more than twenty years, many things about my life changed: furniture, pictures, views from the windows, and even my thoughts. Most surprising of all was that I couldn't stand anything modern anymore. The tumult of urban cultural life behind me, I wanted to bask in the luxury of a beautiful wooded valley rimmed by hazy blue mountains. Perched on its own little hill, my new home reminded me of an alpine spa. Inside, I hankered after objects that looked as if they had existed since the beginning of time. Plexiglas and steel were unthinkable. They had no texture, and no soul.

The local flea markets soon became my Valhalla, a happy hunting ground for anything with a surface that was bleached, mottled, or weathered. I would quite literally jump for joy at the sight of a beautiful patina. Ploughing through piles of Depression glass and random heaps of silverware, I looked for extravagant baubles that called out to me. Perhaps it was an awkwardly lumpish peasant doll from Madeira, with babushka and braids, or a whorled and looping Victorian Christmas ornament made of spun glass, or an eccentric candle in the form of a young cadet with Hamlet haircut, wearing a Scottish kilt and standing at attention.

The business of the treasure hunt gives you an irresistible part to play in the national pageant. Once you really learn to stalk the piles, you may even catch sight of something William Gass describes in *On Being Blue*: you will discover "the love that hides inside of glove, and the ass inside of brass." You may even find "there is dung inside of dungeon" and "pee in perspective." Shopping in flea markets is very much like that. You learn that the things of this world are really containers, and every object is a mythic universe with its own intricate sonorities.

It was only after I became interested in making altars, and created shrewdly placed arrangements for these objects whose evocative soul dramas had stolen their way into my heart, that I discovered a deeper force behind the more mundane motives of shopping and collecting.

An altar is the outcome of many separate acts of attention. Making one affords noble, wild prospects for the soul as an expression of the way we arrange things. An altar is a way of orchestrating passion and articulating acts of perception with the whole being. You can make an inspired one with nothing more than the glow of a single marigold, or your love for an old handmade toy, or the ash heaps generated by prayer. In my case I expect I was, half-consciously, aiming at finding a magnificent obsession, some way to transcend the ordinary. Alone, I wanted to attune my mind to ways of seeing that have remained hidden or left out in our culture. But what I didn't count on, when I made an altar to the Black Madonna, was that it would bring about a stupendous change in my entire life orientation. What I didn't foresee was the peculiar turn my life would take when I discovered, in an unsettling way, that praying to the Black Madonna "works." Or that eventually a sense of faith that wasn't there before would appear, as if in answer to my prayers.

Now, when I light the tiny lamp whose purple shade gives off a smoky violet glow and cross over into oracular space, I signify my intention to live mythically and symbolically. I personalize my belief that the universe is communicating with me in a conscious and intelligent way. In a world that mistrusts and rejects magic, I feel as if I am reclaiming an older, half-forgotten way of consciousness, deep down in the senses. When I probe the realm of spirits, I create opportunities to subtly revise the script my culture has written for me. If my path at this point could claim to be "about" something, this would have to be it: heightening my mystical receptivity to experiences that don't fit into our rationalistic view of the world. "Psychic phenomena are like flowers," writes parapsychologist William Braud, "whose distinctiveness, brightness, beauty, and perfume attract attention, inspire awe, and compel approach." Slowly but surely, I am becoming a psychic gardener. I notice things I never noticed before.

Before I came to Virginia, I didn't have a spiritual path. For as long as I could remember, art was my religion. Growing up in New York City during the salad days of modernism, I belonged to a community of believers whose one true love was art. At eighteen, I was a devotee of John Cage concerts and the avant-garde productions put on stage at the Living Theater. While other girls' minds were filled with boys, proms, and football games, I was translating poetry by Baudelaire and Rimbaud and mingling whenever I could with glamorous artists at the Cedar Bar in Greenwich Village. In those days, Jasper Johns and Robert Rauschenberg were among my closest friends—rarefied macho companions, as solid as redwoods. Several biographers concur that it was I who introduced them to each other, although I don't remember it. I was, in those days, a sophisticated innocent, drawn by the intensity of the New York art world, which defined all of my ambitions, my relationships, my pleasures, and my pains. This was the community in which I felt at home, my urban "family." And though I wasn't yet sure what I wanted to do with myself, I had already figured out there was no future in being an ordinary person.

When I was young I thought I knew what I believed. I never stood back and looked at myself or questioned the habits of the culture that had imprinted me with its particular lures of prestige and power and career success. I lived in a world where ideas mattered. Issues mattered. But I never thought about prayer or having a personal relationship with the divine. In the circles in which I moved, preoccupations like those had less appeal than a rattlesnake's fang.

Much later, when I set out to write my own account of modernism and the art it brought into being, I didn't know I would end up crafting my own private elegy for its mandates. I had no idea that I would need to forsake, as my life progressed, beliefs that I was so well versed in, points of view that were the centerpiece of my entire world. Considering all the things I once took for granted, I sometimes amuse myself now with this thought: what if I had been like Josef Albers, who woke up every day knowing, with sure-footed certainty, that he would paint squares? Then I could have preserved my own traditions without having to court new ones. But life has not been that way for me. I have never stepped twice into the same river.

I didn't experience my first real moment of spiritual aliveness until two days before my fiftieth birthday. I was with about twenty other people on a pilgrimage journey in the Southwest desert, organized by Joan Halifax, a spiritual teacher who blends practices from Buddhist, shamanic, and Native American traditions. We were seated on the ground in a circle, perhaps in an altered state induced by the steady pounding of drums, the rhythmic handclapping and rattling, and the singing of chants. It was late afternoon, but despite the peaceful picture, several people were very tired and on edge. Joan decided to clear a space for healing.

ONE

In one hand, she held a pot of burning sage, and in the other, a white eagle feather that looked like a large white orchid, which had been given to her as a gift from a Native American elder. Moving slowly around the circle with her medicine objects, and shaking her feather, Joan passed wisps of smoke from the burning sage over the energy centers of each person's body, in an attempt to open up places where consciousness and pain were trapped.

When she bent over me, the effect produced by my contact with the feather affected me so intensely that I found myself weeping uncontrollably, releasing, like sparks from every point that was touched, feelings of grief in ecstatic shivers. It was a kind of annunciation, I think now, the vibrational influence of a sacred feather inviting me to my new destiny of reenchantment and opening me, urgently, to the world of myths, symbols, visions, rituals.

After that experience, I never felt the same again about my past or the Western worldview—the rational, scientific conception of reality and the disenchanted philosophy which has shaped the twentieth century by breaking the back of alternative, more magical ways of thinking about life.

By the time I moved to Virginia, I had already had two successful careers, first as an artist making and exhibiting collages, and then as a critic. I had written, most recently, two books that challenged the root metaphor for being an artist in our culture. *The Reenchantment of Art*, published in 1991, the same year I arrived in Virginia, was my attempt to rescue art from a cultural paradigm that privileges masculine attitudes towards reality and mistrusts the feminine. In many ways, what I wrote was outright blasphemy to the world I had grown up in. It was an act of disobedience to canonical presumptions that had been in place for hundreds of years. From that point on, I was no longer a contented product of the old system.

Taking on the patriarchal institutional dragons of art wasn't an easy or comfortable path, yet I never saw myself as cutting the ties to my past. But each of the last three books that I have written has changed my thinking, and this one was no exception. Imperceptibly my life was set on a new path. As a critic I had reached my limits. I had done my best work. I began to see art, and my critical function, as a region I had passed through that had given me a great deal and taught me much but could no longer tempt me to new accomplishments or inspire a fresh outpouring of creative energy. Only now, however, can I see the real reason for this desire to withdraw: an exiled feminine spirit was creating emotional resonance in me, and a hitherto idle and empty part of myself, the spiritual part of my heart and soul, was demanding the right to fulfill itself. This sacred feminine force, springing up everywhere in our culture like a nonstop geyser, is breathing fresh life into rejected modes of consciousness: the psychic, the intuitive, the mystical, and the sacred. Like a wand anointing the mind, it asks us to accept the world as a magical place.

"The soul can work in our lives only through magic," Thomas Moore writes in *The Reenchantment of Everyday Life*. Reenchantment is about putting soul back into the picture. It is about getting the sacred and the secular reembedded in each other. Reenchantment insists on the relational nature of reality—that sense of belonging to a larger pattern. It signifies striking a balance between subjectivity and objectivity, masculine and feminine, discursive and intuitive modes of knowing.

But reenchantment, I now see, demands much more than a critical treatise delivered in the scholar's high tone. More than intellectual lobbying is needed in order to change cultural paradigms that discredit the mystical as being fallacious or fantasy—something that needs to be outgrown. Reenchantment, I have discovered, is a risky personal task: a journey of initiation across an unfamiliar landscape. For if we do not learn it from our own experience—if we cannot teach it to ourselves—then how shall we ever learn it? Surely not from a society crippled by the arrow of unbelief stuck in its own heart.

"If the Goddess is to emerge in our time," writes Jean Shinoda

Bolen in *Crossing to Avalon: A Woman's Midlife Pilgrimage,* "she will do so because women and men tell what they know. The Goddess comes to us in very private experiential ways. To bring about a paradigm shift in the culture that will change assumptions and attitudes, a critical number of us have to tell the stories of our personal revelations and transformations."

We live in a time of stories, of people telling their stories—many of them somber narratives revealing struggles with grim childhoods, addiction, or incest. This book tells the story of how an encounter with the divine feminine has happened in my life. Not as a single anomalous occurrence, but as a complex of enigmatic and beguiling experiences suggesting a pattern with an apparent purpose that is often beyond my reckoning, and seems to come out of a place there's no explaining. After a lifetime of writing about others and their work, the thought of writing about myself—of seeing my own reflection in the pool—was not what I expected. Indeed, it had not occurred to me, until I began pursuing a path with the Black Madonna, that I, too, had a story to tell.

Two

LIKE many others, I was first drawn to the Black Madonna through the books of Marion Woodman, a renowned Jungian writer. According to Woodman, images of the Black Madonna are erupting in the hearts and minds of many individuals today, often through dreams, demanding conscious recognition. Mythically, the Black Madonna speaks to the need in the West to reintegrate the feminine and the mystical into consciousness. Because of this, I approached her as a pivotal icon, a representation of everything for which I have striven in my own writing.

In my case, the Black Madonna didn't appear to me in a dream. One day I was walking around in the shopping area of downtown Santa Barbara when I noticed an unusual religious statue through the plate-glass window of a gift store. It was a carved, wooden, female *Santos* from the Philippines, about two feet high, and it was not really black, but more the color of bitumen or pewter, a graying wood that had lost its original coat of paint. To my eye the figure emanated the spirit of the Black Madonna. I couldn't help but buy it, in a flight of cosmic fancy, although I had no idea at the time that my relationship with this mercurial icon would one day become a conduit for the unfolding of a powerful mythic journey in my life.

People often ask me: who, or what, is the Black Madonna? They want to know why I am attracted to her. The answer is that she helps me to do the work I most love. She is teaching me the art of magical connection. We are born to be mystics, suggests Caroline Myss, a pioneer in the field of energy medicine and human consciousness. Our biology is wired for it. In our culture, however, this becomes something of a liability. The fact that divine mystery is at odds with our culture's scientific bias is what makes its pursuit so forbidding. Now that I recognize how the acceptance of the world as a magical place shapes human awareness in a particular way, I can also see the possibility for whole cultures and civilizations to be changed and renewed, even turned upside down, by individuals who undergo certain powerful experiences and retain enough stability and sanity to tell about it.

There are some four hundred Black Madonnas throughout the world, located mostly in Europe. The most well known, probably, are Our Lady of Czestochowa in Poland and Notre Dame de Montserrat in Spain. During the Middle Ages, a number of chivalric and heretical cults, such as the troubadours of Provence, the Knights Templar (a Crusading order of warrior-monks), and the Cathars (an ascetic Christian sect that rejected the authority of the Roman Catholic Church) venerated the moral and spiritual authority of the divine feminine. During the medieval civilization of the twelfth and thirteenth centuries, according to *L'Énigme des vierges noires*, a little known book written by a French lawyer, Jacques Huynen, who did extensive research to uncover "the enigma of the Black Virgins," Black Madonnas were placed in cathedrals that celebrated the cult of "Notre Dame." They were the central inspirational icons of pilgrimage and were connected with miraculous visions and cures.

The icons were often found in underground grottoes or crypts, built on old Druidic sites associated with dolmens, magnetic earth currents, or healing springs. It is thought that the monastic elites, mystery school initiates, and adepts of alchemy used these honeycombed vaults in the great Gothic cathedrals to do their work, and that this underground stream of Western heresy was undoubtedly the nerve center, the spiritual switchboard, for the worship of the divine feminine. Many of the original icons were destroyed during the Inquisition in the twelfth century, because the Black Madonna's supremacy was threatening to the male-only authority of the

Roman Catholic priesthood. Precious documents that might have told us more about the esoteric significance of the Black Madonna were also destroyed at that time. Today the greatest concentration of Black Madonnas is in the Auvergne region of France.

Unlike the "white" Virgin Mary, the Black Madonna is often portrayed as a queen, an archetype of powerful femininity. She can be quite fierce, as is the Indian goddess Kali, who is typically black and wears a necklace of skulls—and whose distended red tongue, almost intolerably grotesque, reaches down to touch her chin. White virgins embody the "white" virtues: purity, innocence, submission, and moral restraint. Blackness expresses a different chemistry altogether, related to the *nigredo*, or blackening stage of death and decay, in alchemical transformation.

Originally her dark color was attributed to the effects of candle smoke in the chapel, or to discoloration resulting from dampness in the grottoes. Today we understand that this was a myth to cover up her pagan ancestry, and her pre-Christian roots in the cult of Black Isis, which was a powerful rival to Christianity in the Middle Ages. According to Luisah Teish, a Yoruba priestess who writes about the Black Madonna of Guadalupe, we should not be bamboozled by the candle-smoke story. Theologians, she says, are fond of claiming that Black Virgins found in Europe were not originally black. "They love to say that the statues were charred during a fire in the church or that some vandal painted the face as a way of disgracing the Church. This is so much bullshit. It is, I feel, a neurotic attempt on the part of the Vatican to deny Mother Africa and the dark races as the foreparents of humanity."

The fact is, nobody really knows for sure why the Black Madonna is black. The blackness is part of her mystery, and no perfunctory summary can do justice to her profoundly mysterious character. When Christianity took over the Black Madonna from antiquity, her occult qualities were expunged. She was conflated with the Virgin Mary and left out of the Trinity. Her reemergence today signifies a new blueprint trying to emerge in human consciousness. Symbolically, the Black Madonna is healing that part of mass consciousness that has been victimized by patriarchy.

For several years after I got my Black Madonna, I didn't know what to do with her. At first, I had only a rudimentary altar for the Madonna in my new home. I placed her on a turquoise Mexican table in front of the living room window, where she stood looking for all the world like a Manchu prophetess, with an embroidered tortilla cloth under her feet. On either side of her were two candles set in cobalt blue glass holders, with a scattering of birds' nests and a bleached-out turtle shell at her feet.

But as time passed, the door to a deeper world opened. Today she is a virtuoso performance, a flamboyant fantasia, festooned to the hilt with trailing charms, jewels, amulets, and carnival beads. Red and blue glass rosaries hang from her neck, along with a pink brocade medicine bundle, a routine good-luck charm from Japan. Layered down the length of her long body are clusters of old Christmas bells, green parrot feathers, a Native American spirit-catcher, two orange jade rings, in the shape of lifesavers, brought back by a friend from Beijing, and an opalescent glass swan, the color of crushed strawberries. Trussed into this planktonlike net shrouding the Madonna is an ivory Shiela-na-gig, a rather forbidding Celtic deity found in the entry arches of old Irish churches, whose knees point outward and whose feet press inward at the soles, exposing a protruding vulva.

One of the more dazzling aspects of having an altar is how alive it is. Adding a new object always reveals new layers of subliminal influence to the plot. Whether it is the folded prayer bundle from Tibet, encased in colored yarn, or the droll little elf in a pea-green witch's hat, sitting on a silver mesh moon, playing the cymbals— my favorite Christmas ornament—I treasure every scrap of her peacocked garb, packed with offerings given by other people: the tiny fragment of red felt, for example, that arrived by mail one year at Christmas from an artist I never met, alleged to be from the original coat of Santa Claus. There is the miniature jingle bell from a Buddhist temple in Japan that belonged to Teeny Duchamp, Marcel Duchamp's widow, an amulet which her daughter Jackie sent to me after she died; the good-luck charm brought back from Jerusalem by my friend Estill, a vertical row of seven indigo-blue glass elephants, each one slightly larger than the previous one; and the tiny baby-bunting, immaculately asleep in one half of a walnut shell, that Betty found in Budapest.

At the Black Madonna's feet, as if an old wizard had emptied his pockets there, is an assortment of crystals, trade beads, seed pods, milagros, figurines, and dried flowers, becoming, in their opulent decay, more faded and powdery every day. I like to look upon this wonderful, crumbling mess as my spiritual compost pile.

My friend Paulus Berensohn, a potter who loves in Penland, North Carolina, recently installed a "greeting" altar outside his house. When a visitor is due to arrive, Paulus lights a candle and puts out two cups of cognac. I love the lyrical grace of this gesture, the warmth at its core. Paulus claims that altars need to be reinvented for our time. In the last few years, many people have turned to private altars as a way of communing with the divine, without the intermediary of organized religion. When I ask Paulus what the purpose of having altars is for him, he takes on the air of someone wrapt in thought.

"I need in my life to be constantly reminded," he says, "and the altar works as a kind of crossing point for me between the obsessions of my own life and the living world. That's why I have altars all over my house: to constantly remind me of who else is here. The altar becomes this place of altering my consciousness, of opening my consciousness to include the spiritual dimension." But mostly, he says, it's a place for exercising the "technology of gratitude." It's a place to offer thanks and praise.

A few years ago while in Hawaii, Paulus discovered a social ritual that he really liked. When Hawaians go visiting, they will often wrap up a stone in some expressive way as a token of friendship and offer it as a gift.

"Stones are very spiritual objects," says Paulus, reaching deep inside his pocket. "I always carry one with me, and when I need healing, when I need to remind myself, I take out my stone, and I hold my stone."

Three

SPECULATING on the proprieties of autobiography, the poet James Merrill once raised the question: "Who needs the full story of any life?" Certainly the essence of any life—all that it has gained and lost—can be extracted in different ways, as much from its deep "implicate order" as from its concrete surface. Still, slicing to get to the heart of the matter is harder than it looks.

Once I decided to write about my life, I raided my old diaries and notebooks, hoping to find some iridescent shards that might be germane to the task. It grieves me to report that they are hopelessly irregular, and peter out altogether by the end of the 1970s. Clearly I was no Leonard Woolf, who thrived on keeping scrupulous accounts of the miles he drove, the date he had his hair cut, and the dates of his wife's periods. But taking stock of the random pieces did produce this cumulative self-revelation: I was not exactly a frumpy, provincial Miss Mouse either, living life at low wick and surviving mostly on boiled eggs. Amid the patient writing of books, I often found myself a guest at large, happy parties—with much celebratory eating and dancing on the walls. I lived in a world quite different from the one I live in now. As a necessary prelude to my present life, I offer these few chosen glimpses of myself in the decades before I arrived in Virginia—not from self-aggrandizing necessity, but more in the way of poetic truth—as one might share images of one's younger self, preserved in a photo album.

I'd have to say that for many years, Jasper Johns was, in fact, my Fred Astaire, the person in whose company I was always happiest. Over the course of three decades, he was as central to my life as his work has been to American art. Jasper and I met before he became famous; he was living in a loft at the bottom of Manhattan, and working as a sales clerk at the Marlboro bookstore on West 57th Street. A mutual friend introduced us. I was instantly drawn to his luminous melancholy, his icicle wit, and his outrageous laugh.

One Christmas holiday, Jasper invited me to visit him at his house in St. Martin, in the French West Indies. We sat under the lime and grapefruit trees in his garden on Christmas Eve, conversing about whether anybody has ever investigated ugliness with the same passion that people are irresistibly drawn to think about beauty. It was quite hot and I was thrilled to be spending Christmas in my bikini. Jasper and I were reading aloud to each other from a book—Francine du Plessix Gray's recently published memoir, *Lovers and Tyrants*—both of us doubled over with laughter and literally howling at a comment produced by her French lover as Francine removes her necklace before getting into bed: "There is something fabulously seductive about the clang of real pearls upon the night table, good for an immediate erection."

The next day, listening to the Savannah Band play *"Cherchez la Femme"* and Elkie Brook sing "Love Potion No. 9," Jasper was making breadcrumbs from dry bread in the blender. Impetuously he pushed all the buttons at once—crumb, shred, grate, blend, etc. Feeling a bit impetuous myself, I tried to get him to wear my pearl necklace to lunch. He refused.

"It has too many innuendoes," he said, looking suddenly sober.

Another time, in France, we were hunting for mushrooms in the forest of Fontainebleau with Teeny Duchamp and her daughter Jackie. I was arm-in-arm with Jasper, who doggedly recited the whole of Edith Sitwell's *Façade* to me by heart, imitating perfectly her rapid falsetto and making me laugh so hard I could hardly walk.

Another time, on a snowy day in New York, Jasper came to visit me wearing a beautiful white sweater his mother had knitted for him. The first time he ever saw snow, he informed me, was in South Carolina, where he grew up, at the age of five.

THREE

"Were you excited?" I asked.

"Oh yes, everyone was," he replied. "We collected the snow in cardboard boxes and then ate it with oranges and brandy."

Months later I reminded him of this story, and he looked incredulous.

"Brandy?" he whooped. "At five years old? I must have been wrong about the brandy."

On another occasion, during a weekend spent at his country house in Stony Point, New York, we passed the time reading aloud to each other from Iris Murdoch's novel, *The Sacred and Profane Love Machine*. At the end of the afternoon, Jasper gathered a clump of ratty looking mushrooms from the base of a tree stump near the house. To my great discomfort, he cooked them up for supper, together with a baked sweet potato.

"That's dinner," he announced petulantly. It was his way of drubbing me, because earlier I'd vetoed the purchase of a packet of pork chops in the supermarket.

In London in 1978, I put on my prized purple and blue wool string jacket for an opening of Jasper's retrospective at the Hayward Gallery and stood before him. He rolled his eyes at me in that way he does. Then, his face wreathed in smiles, he said I looked just like an orangutan.

After the opening, there was a party in his honor at someone's house not far from my neighborhood. We were walking home, late, and Jasper, who was a little drunk, wanted to play "Wittgenstein's game," which, he explained, really needs three people—one to take the part of the sun, and one to take the parts, respectively, of the moon and the earth. The earth runs around the sun, the moon runs around the earth, and the sun runs in a straight line. Soon I was hurtling down Connaught Street with Jasper orbiting around me, both of us hoarse from laughing so hard. We passed a man standing in a doorway, his arms laden with packages, and tried to coax him into playing the third part, but he refused.

Jasper and I had a conversation once about the composer Leonard Bernstein, whom Jasper viewed as primarily interested in power and pushing his way to the top. Most people, he conceded, are interested in those things, but in Bernstein's case, it seemed more flagrant. I asked Jasper how he felt, himself, about having power. He paused briefly, then answered.

"It's something I'd like to have, but I'd prefer that it was given to me. I don't want to work at trying to get it."

On another occasion, he was planning to leave New York for his house in St. Martin. When I asked if he would be gone for some time, he read me the riot act. The question irked him and it elicited a classic "Jasper" response.

"You can't go away for no time, because then I'd be staying here."

Then there was the moment when I spoke these words of deep feeling, but only to my diary: "You are the most attractive, amusing, and dearest friend anyone ever had." The sentiment corresponded perfectly to a line in a Judy Collins' song at the time: "I'm so glad to see you my friend, you're like the rainbow, comin' round the bend." It's what I felt, but I knew better than to ever say the words out loud. A friend in those days, Edwin Schlossberg, once made a first-person statement to Jasper.

"I really love you," Eddie said.

"That's your problem," came the terse but instructive reply as the eyes rolled again.

For more than twenty years, during the 1970s and '80s, I went every summer to a small fishing village on the coast of Catalonia, called Cadaqués. The town was right on the Mediterranean, north of Barcelona. Salvador Dali had a house there. Once I was taken along by some people to one of his afternoon "*darshans*," when he would receive visitors seated under an olive tree in his walled garden. Surrounding him on this particular afternoon were numerous hippies and his current new love, Amanda—a man who had undergone a sex-change operation, and was dressed up in a black satin gown and black gloves, which were elbow length but had no fingers. Amanda's voice was very *basso*; her hair, the glittering ash-blond of a Rhine-maiden. Music slid into the room from somewhere—the soundtrack from *A Clockwork Orange*, one of Dali's favorite films.

I was wearing my Magritte button—the image of a bowler-hatted man with a green apple in front of his face—a deliberate provocation meant to display my allegiance. Dali noticed it immediately.

"*Viva* Magritte," he said to me with a grin, and then turned away, perceiving no merit in conversing any further.

After an hour or so, glasses of sparkling pink champagne mysteriously appeared on a tray. Then Dali excused himself. He needed to go and change clothes, because he and Amanda were invited out to dinner. She suggested that he dress in white.

"Ah, because you are all in black," came the instant reply, "and then we can be dominoes. *Je ferai le tout possible*." He did his best, and reappeared a short time later, looking pure as the driven snow.

There were other idiosyncratic surrealist adventures as well. One night in New York I was invited to meet Leonora Carrington and Meret Oppenheim—two vintage surrealist *grandes dames*, supercharged, in their way, with mythic history. In those days, I used to wear tea rose perfume and smoke Indian beedees. I don't know whose house it was, but when I got there, the scene was definitely odd, like seeing something in slow motion, with about ten people loosely sprawled on the floor, some with their eyes closed. Suddenly Leonora (who, it must be said, had a history of episodes of clinical madness) appeared from the kitchen and said, "Shall we try the muffins now?" Only, there weren't any muffins. Then she said, as if impelled to communicate some pressingly important piece of information: "I rushed in and lived with him, and then rushed out again. The giant mandrill in the Bronx."

For several years, during the time I was in London, I was good friends with the painter Francis Bacon. One night, I went to an expensive restaurant in Bloomsbury with Francis and John Russell, an English art critic with whom I was living at the time. John was writing a book about Bacon, so we saw him often. When dinner arrived, Francis, who was flagrantly drunk, took an instant dislike to the sauce covering his fish. Tilting his plate off the edge of the table, he peevishly drained the liquid onto the floor, making a mess on the fancy carpet. Several waiters rushed immediately to his side, flapping over him as if he were a chicken who had just laid an egg.

In Langhan's Bistro one night, we had a conversation about friendship. Francis lamented that he didn't see his friends Lucian Freud or Peter Beard any more. "Friendships have a life span," he said ruefully, "and they die."

When I alluded to my own misguided tendency to try to make a best friend of everyone I like, he looked at me wide-eyed. "But it's your best quality," he mused.

Francis complained on another occasion that the writer Iris Murdoch kept sending him invitations to meet in a pub, which he consistently refused. "I don't think she's my type," he said, flashing his wicked, drawled grin.

Early on in my relationship with John Russell, we visited the painter Balthus, best known for his strange groupings of pubescent girls in sexual trance. John was curating an exhibition of Balthus's work for the Tate Gallery, which was the reason for the invitation to spend a weekend at his Roman villa. I had no part in this scenario, but was taken along for the ride. From the moment we arrived, Balthus never addressed a single word to me. Deprived of any identity, I felt like an undesirable who gets turned away at the border. But this was not the only example of Balthus's studied remoteness. When he wanted to smoke, he telephoned to a servant who was on another floor of the house to bring him his cigarettes—which were sitting on a table across the room—so he would not have to get up and get them himself.

Life in those days wasn't all dancing and Chinese lanterns and champagne in torrents, however, and spending long hours in the company of favorites. I was living in a world where it was fatal not to make one's mark, and there were times when I would tremble

THREE

under the awning of inadequacy. In 1974, John left me quite suddenly and went to New York to live with someone else. I felt sandbagged with a sense of undigested pain, and was brooding a lot. From my diary of that year:

> I've been wandering through life these last weeks with the aimlessness of a fly buzzing about a windowpane, tormented by a sense that I have failed to make my life work. It's a kind of cliff-hanging that I do periodically when everything seems as if it is going wrong. I wish there were some cure for such states of malaise and despair—the way ladybirds were once prescribed and eaten in large numbers as a cure for measles. What one needs most in such moments is exactly what one has least of: faith that the world will indeed open up again, resplendent, and in the shape of a streaming chrysanthemum.

I suppose that kind of archetypal whistling in the dark is common to everyone on their desperate days. Mine always seemed to arrive on bank holidays in London. On one of those weekends, I was feeling particularly lonely and sorry for myself. I had recently returned from a lecture tour in India, where I saw thousands of people living in misery on the streets, brushing their teeth using the dirty water from puddles. I told myself, after that experience, that I would give up every form of humbug and would never complain about anything again. And I meant it. But then I heard David Hockney remark—we were all together at a friend's house in Clapham for dinner—that London was an impossibly lonely place for people who were living on their own. David announced his decision to move to America that night, where, he said, he's never lonely, never down.

Hockney's way of adjusting down from loneliness was to keep his pockets full of cigars and his conversation packed with an extravagant flow of outlandish jokes. Did you hear about the leper who threw his hand in at cards? Or about the fortune teller who broke his leg tomorrow? Eventually David moved to California, where he found himself a wonderful old house on the beach in

Malibu. Some time after that I moved, too, leaving the cachet of fashionable life pretty much behind me. I washed up in rural Virginia, with big black crows cawing in the sky overhead.

A friend, writing to me from London recently, pointed out that, encrypted in the name of my adoptive town, Blacksburg, Virginia, are the words "Black Virgin." No doubt an exceedingly interesting roll of the dice has landed me here. Synchronicity, casting its shadow on my circumstances, is how the deeper order ignites on the surface.

Four

SIGNIFICANT mythic journeys often begin when the very act of seeking sets something in motion to meet us. Something in the universe responds, as if to an invitation.

Once I was settled in my home in Virginia, with two leather armchairs soft as soap facing each other and Beethoven's "Moonlight" sonata rippling through the room, I felt the way Dorothy must have felt when she finally arrived in Oz. Except that when I looked about, I found that I was alone, deeply and viscerally alone.

My life has always been strong in every area except love, to a point where I had begun to suspect that fate was against it. From the beginning I have never been able to fit myself into the conventional narrative of marriage and motherhood. With the exception of the six-year happy interlude when I lived with John Russell, I have rarely enjoyed the luxury of being half a couple. Most of my achievements in the professional world have been done in the absence of male companionship. Still, I was not yet ready to resign myself irredeemably to this shortfall, and had never really given up a gentle, backward longing to one day inhabit that other world of people who are not alone.

Perhaps it was the empty armchair, tactfully beckoning me to seek out this "missing" energy; I'm not really sure. But my heart was suddenly my gripped by a desire to penetrate love's mystery, so that it would teach me its secrets. I imagined placing my cheek against somebody's palm. It was as if bandits had suddenly come down from the hills, bearing a fireball.

What if I were to try and enlist the Black Madonna's help to draw a passionate companion into my life? Would she respond? Do I truly believe that the Black Madonna has the power to make this happen? If I do this, I will be joining in spirit with a long line of pilgrims who, over the ages, have prayed beside the statue of a saint, offering it a *milagro* or other gift, in order to obtain supernatural help to cure a sickness or solve a problem. Can I give myself to the Black Madonna as wholeheartedly as these pilgrims?

One evening I light the votive candles on my altar, and with a little paper petition cloistered in my hand, ask for help in manifesting a man of courage—someone who will embody the masculine energy of the spiritual warrior. I am not looking for an ordinary relationship, but for one which would be chosen and revealed through the path of the heart. "Let others think what they like," José Ortega y Gasset wrote in his essay *On Love*; "for me, the culmination of life consists of a pure and subtly dramatic passion. Not everyone falls in love, nor do those capable of falling in love fall in love with just anyone." I have never done anything like this before. Although it doesn't occur to me at this point to doubt what I am doing, I know instinctively that there are no guarantees. Whatever happens, happens; I will have to be satisfied, even if it is nothing.

Several months pass. Sometimes things have to cook for a while, before anything starts to emerge, and the little miracles begin to happen. I am traveling by car with a friend in California, when we decide to stop briefly at a roadside antiques fair in the town of Santa Rosa. The quality of weekend fairs fluctuates drastically, and this one does not yield anything of interest. We are on the way out, when the ticket vendor at the front door points out a side room that we have missed. It turns out to be filled with tribal and shamanic artifacts from all over the world. I am immediately excited, almost as if I had stepped out of time and into an Ice Age cave in the Lascaux hills.

Nestled beside a group of small crystal Buddhas, I discover a piece of religious art—a Tibetan tantric dagger, carved in wood the color of tobacco leaf. It has three enigmatic male faces engraved on the handle, with strips of beige and sea-green rag bandaged around its neck, indicating previous use in some kind of ritual activity.

The symbolic purpose of the dagger, according to the man who sells it to me, is to pierce through deeper and deeper levels of illusion, a practice serving a transformational function in the Buddhist tradition. I decide to take the dagger home and offer it to the Black Madonna to implement my *manda*. In the tradition of the *manda*, you bind yourself to your icon by a promise or a gift (usually in the form of a *milagro*). I have been waiting for the right offering to show itself, and as I hold the dagger with its hypnotic, frayed bandages, I know I have found it.

While he is wrapping up the dagger, the dealer suggests I might try to sleep with it next to my pillow, in order to induce a potent dream. That night, on a lark, I do what he tells me to do. I put the dagger on my pillow and unexpectedly dream about Tom, the man with whom I have been studying Tai Chi and other Chinese internal martial arts for more than a year.

The dream unsettles me. It has a tenuous erotic quality that is almost invisible, just like the movements in Tai Chi. Implausible as it seems at the time, the feeling which accompanies these erotic movements is ecstatic. For a fleeting moment, Tom and I are like two pure mirrors facing each other. And then I wake up.

Put bluntly, I had never considered this maverick loner, who is rather distant and bristling, as a romantic presence in my life. It's not that I didn't find him attractive—I did—especially the manganese gray-blue eyes like subterranean stone, and the long dark hair floating down in wisps and scraps below his shoulders like a fishing line. But Tom seemed more like a shy animal on the outskirts of the human settlement than a likely candidate for love. He was touchy, just like those Mongolian horses I once read about who were half wild and difficult to saddle up. Although they were tough and could run really fast, they were easily spooked. Even shadows cast by a campfire set them bucking. A sneeze could a start a stampede. In his loneliness, this man, I knew, was just like that.

But I enjoyed his bladelike humor, and especially his stories. During the year or so that I had been taking his class, Tom and I had often had breakfast together. He liked going to a certain greasy-spoon restaurant near the dojo, not the local café with decaf mochas, bagels, and spongy muffins, and he always sat facing the door (not trusting his back to anyone) and ordered the identical breakfast: two BLTs on toast and a glass of iced tea. Without ice.

Tom had a harsh, unfiltered quality to his being that intrigued me. Sometimes I thought of ancient hunter-gatherers of the northern forests who skied across the frozen lakes on polished animal bones. Conversation tended to be impersonal, on lively topics like coal mining, a subject in which he was well-versed, having grown up in western Virginia in a small coal-mining town called Grundy. His uncle was the mayor of Grundy and ran the town for many years. Tom left Grundy to go to college at Virginia Tech, studying physics and psychology—after which he settled down in Blacksburg permanently and bought several houses. He rented rooms to students and taught Tai Chi, his real passion. He has studied it all over the world, including mainland China.

I soon learned that Tai Chi wasn't aerobics. It was a way of life. To study it from a master is to find yourself being subtly changed in profound ways. You come to identify with the principles of perfect action, repeating the same form through practice until you succeed in creating smooth, effortless movement. Tom liked to tout the fact that he had been wearing the same pair of Kung Fu shoes day and night for a decade, with no visible deterioration of the soles.

He also liked to regale me with tales of his Kung Fu studies in Taiwan with his American teacher. In the afternoons, after working out, they would rendezvous at a café in a section of town known as "Snake Alley." Basically it was a warren filled with hundreds of writhing snakes. Visitors could choose the particular snake they wanted, then it would be killed while you watched. Then you would be served the heart to eat, and the blood and venom to drink.

Stories like this would prickle my scalp when I heard them. Part of me saw Tom as a man of hidden fires, but the other part thinks he is a cold fish. Now, in the light of my odd dream, I found myself wondering whether this fierce and guarded warrior-monk, who drank snake's blood as if it were grape juice and could walk across rice paper without leaving a footprint, would ever allow the complications of love into his life. Clearly a man more comfortable with swords than with valentines, Tom seemed secure in his isolation, free of dependency and weakness. Would he ever enter the hazardous terrain of women? I couldn't picture him wearing a fitted suit or marching off into the sunset with a lady. If what I wanted was to be swept away, surely this had to be a losing proposition. How could he be the Black Madonna's answer to my prayers?

I arrive home from California the next day, to find a message on my answering machine. It was Tom, announcing that he had bought a copy of the Sunday *New York Times* and was holding it for me, in case I had failed to get one. Nothing like this has ever happened with him before, and the fact that he doesn't feel the need to identify himself seems particularly unusual. My intuition flares at the unanticipated sound of his voice with its odd message, and the meshing with my dream from the night before. Something breaks the frame of my perception, and in that moment, I understood that somewhere, a train was quietly sliding out of the station.

Tom and I begin to see more of each other after my return from California, but it takes me a while to understand that I can't just see where I am headed and go there. In fact, instead of a relationship, gradually I find myself in a labyrinth: a difficult and confusing situation, filled with trials and obstacles that tested not only my will, but my personal limitations as well. As the poet Rainer Maria Rilke once wrote, "the future must enter into you a long time before it happens."

All labyrinths embody the principle of delay. (James Joyce

suggested three hundred years for the penetration of *Finnegan's Wake*.) Waiting became my task. Waiting, in a situation that would remain liminal, on the threshold between the worlds and not fully present in my life, until an old self could die—the one dedicated to protective gestures and the power of self-sufficiency—and a new identity could be formed. "Rare women," D. H. Lawrence wrote in *The Man Who Died*, "wait for the reborn man." Ultimately each of us bets our life on some picture of reality. And then, we stand or fall by that choice. Eventually we learn that there is no controlling the speed at which things happen in our lives.

In my case, there isn't much to go on. Everything Tom does, I discover, is done in Taoist fashion, with hints and suggestions only—a nod or a handshake rather than a written contract. Everything could be taken in a double way. Everything was hard to figure out, unless you learned to read a set of tricky footprints in the dark.

For example, one day Tom gives me a large, highly technical volume, *Fundamentals of Chinese Medicine*, from his library. He doesn't explain what it is for, but it is certainly not for the beautiful absurdity of my ever trying to read it. On two occasions when I offer to return the book, he wants me to continue to keep it. Finally I understand that what I am really holding is an intention of some kind, the little red dot on the map where Tom has, so to speak, "booked" himself in. It was the subtlest of claims—assuming, of course, that my interpretation was right.

But is it? There is never any knowing for certain. At the heart of the labyrinth is the energy of uncertainty: uncertainty about the outcome, and in my case, uncertainty about the whole nature of an enterprise in which there is a great contradiction between something that seems to be happening, yet isn't.

Some of the labyrinth's paths are dead ends. Getting out requires a series of correct choices. These two Draconian components of my situation, delay and uncertainty, lead me to consult the *I Ching*, an ancient Chinese oracle system that Jung used for over thirty years, for help. I am trying to gain insight beyond my conscious understanding that might help me.

"Because your new environment has yet to wholly materialize, much confusion surrounds any attempt to master it. Hold to your own center and allow fate to manipulate external events. If you persevere a great success is at hand. Retreat from the inner demand that either the situation improve or you will abandon it. Keep going forward, accepting the situation as it is, without bemoaning your fate. Beyond the difficulties and pressures that surround you, a success lies waiting."

I enter a period of daily divinations. My readings from the *I Ching* (a synthesis from five different versions of the text) strongly affect how I see my situation. When I listen to the oracle, I can stay charged and purposeful. I can fly outside the box of ordinary thinking—and my habitual responses of doubt and mistrust that might otherwise cause me to cancel, dump, or airlift this obstinate loner out of my life. My oracular readings fill me with a confidence that is unwarranted by the facts of the situation.

"Cling to the possibility of a positive outcome in the situation that faces you, no matter how unlikely it may seem. An outward situation will come to an end in time. What is important now is to remain united in your heart with another. Although it costs a severe struggle to overcome the obstacles, the path leads back to happiness."

But what if this directive encouragement is unreliable? What if I am hunting for bones in a cream puff? If I continue to hang in there, will I just be setting myself up for some terrible disappointment?

Five

AN INVITATION arrives from the executive director of the Art Museum of Western Virginia, Joanne Kuebler, to hear a lecture by Robert Farris Thompson. Thompson, a professor of art history at Yale University, is perhaps the most eminent contemporary authority on African art, having written several books which describe the impact of Africa on the cultures of North and South America.

When I get the invitation, none of this rings any bells. Joanne, however, insistent that I come, assures me that Thompson is a prodigious speaker, filled with spiritual, personal, and poetic passion for his subject. As a result of her urging, I decide to go.

Even the preliminary sales pitch has not prepared me for the dramatic effect of this somewhat dandified man in his sixties, gray-haired and bespectacled and wearing a business suit, talking intimately about native traditions. Thompson punctuates his speech with African phrases, spoken forcefully and brilliantly, with a very particular emotion. I soon realize that he doesn't just talk *about* African culture, he *transmits* it, like a tribesman fanning himself in the steamy heat—and then he literally *steps* into it, dancing animatedly on stage as he ends his talk with a tape of mambo music.

When white people hear this music, he tells the audience, they think it belongs in a dance hall. But black people know "this is church!" To underline his point, Thompson pivots around and declares, "We're calling down spirits here." The emblematic essence of a whole culture has just been set loose in the room.

This man isn't afraid of anything. I am utterly seduced and the whole experience challenges me to rethink the possibilities of the lecture form. No more old-fashioned academic set pieces. Thompson has crossed a threshold into another reality. From this place, discourse can be electric and kinesthetic. It can cast a spell.

Joanne has told me that Thompson knows my work and is interested in meeting me. At the reception afterwards, I venture a few words in his direction, but there is no sign of recognition. So I am surprised early the next morning when Joanne calls to say that they are headed in this direction and would like to come by for a visit. Thompson wants to check out an example of "yard art" in Christiansburg that he's heard about—for veiled Yoruba influences. He also wants to see my Black Madonna altar.

An hour before they arrive, Ray Kass, a local artist, calls and reminds me that Thompson was the curator of an exhibition of African-American altars, called "The Face of the Gods," which I saw when it was on view at the Center for African Art in New York in 1993. (Later, the exhibition traveled to other museums around the country.) I belatedly realize I am about to spend a morning with the world's most knowledgeable expert on altars.

As Joanne's car pulls into my driveway, this intense, eccentric, dramatically entertaining man climbs out and walks straight over to where I am standing. Then he plants a kiss right on my lips. "You never told me your name," he explains, "so I didn't know who you were." Somehow, huddled in the crowd of admirers after the lecture, I had failed to properly introduce myself.

We move inside to my altar. Thompson studies it for a while, and I can see that it makes an impression on him. In the Kongo-Cuban-Yoruba traditions, it is customary to show one's appreciation for the power of the gods by offering a "sacrifice." Thompson reaches into his pocket, and drops four quarters at the Black Madonna's feet.

As we drive off to look for "yard art," Thompson and I talk in the back seat of the car. I ask him if his involvement with altars has come about through his interest in African cultures.

"It came about through the fact that I've been initiated," he replies. And then, hinting at some personal secrecy, Thompson confides that he has an altar at home to Erinle, the Nigerian god of hunting and water, a Christlike figure who once sacrificed himself so that others would have water to drink during a terrible drought. Few people ever see the altar, however, because it's hidden away in his bedroom.

"It's only because you have an altar, too, that I'm telling you about it," he says. "In the Yoruba-Cuban world, which now includes a lot of Miami and a lot of New York, there is *la question de las cameras*, the question of rooms. Because when you say the word 'room,' it's meant to be underlined, since it refers to secret rooms, where sacred stuff is kept. Usually now, it's the innermost bedroom. Traditionally it would have been the innermost part of the forest, the inner grove. But now you don't have a forest anymore."

Thompson also reveals that he consults his altar, that it has divination equipment—a set of cowrie shells, which, he says is not unlike consulting the *I Ching*. The Yoruba have a divination system called "Ifa," but you have to know how to interpret the answer after you throw the shells, Thompson warns.

I ask about "The Face of the Gods" exhibition. It seems that Thompson invited some of his personal friends, Yoruba priests and priestesses, to make altars especially for the show. The most dramatic altar was created as an offering to a strong Kongo spirit called Sarabanda, a sort of John Henry figure, who worked on the railroads in Cuba. This particular altar had to have iron vessels, iron horseshoes, and big railroad nails of the type that binds the ties together. It also had to be fed rum, daily. The museum staff rolled their eyes over this, according to Thompson. "Why don't you let it all happen?" he told them.

This altar was so authentic that it drew "sacrifice" from people in the Kongo-Cuban tradition, dropped in the form of coins and dollar bills. At each installation site, the altars accrued about five hundred dollars in small change.

"What do we do with the money?" the museum staff wanted to know. Thompson told them that since it was "sacrifice," they should give it away to something worthy, so the money was given to a hospital for children with AIDS.

Rather bluntly, one person came up to him and said, "Oh, I think these things look so antiseptic in a museum. Obviously they're out of context." Choosing his moment carefully, while none of the guards were looking, Thompson invited the woman to do a little *"frottage,"* by rubbing her fingers along the surface of a big iron bird that was gleaming with honey and myrrh and other sacred substances.

"Oh, this is very sticky—it's alive!" she cried, quickly withdrawing her hand.

"Yeah!" Thompson answered, hardly concealing his delight. "All of the altars have something like that hidden in them."

Each of the altars had been consecrated ritually and was "fed" continuously during the show. Some people within the African-American community even used them for meditation and prayer. The tradition of working altars had seeped right into the museum setting, and had simply molded the experience to its own purposes. Thompson remembered some comments from a museum guard's notes: "10:30. Person kneeling and meditating. What should I do? 11:30. Woman comes in and deposits apples. These might bring rats. What should I do?"

The biggest problem he had in spinning out this vision, according to Thompson, was with the "museum mentality." Many staff members felt some discomfort about exhibiting working altars in a museum. To counter their misgivings, Thompson suggested they bring the priests and priestesses together and ask them, in a plain way, how they felt about having their altars on display in a museum. The priests and priestesses responded that, because their religions have been so maligned by white, Western culture and disparaged as being "voodoo," they welcomed the opportunity to bring their most potent instrument, the altar, into a museum.

"They saw immediately that a museum is a dignifying machine, that when you put something into a museum, it's a way of saying 'This is worthwhile, this is a tradition.' I was aware of that, they were aware of it, and we just closed ranks." Of course, the whole thing could have gone the other way, if someone had been hung up on alienating terms like the "Other." But, as Thompson points out, these Yoruba priests and priestesses weren't the "Other"—they were his friends. "We just did it as a quiet thing among friends."

Like Thompson's altar-makers, I am about to remove my altar from the serenity of my living room and take it on the road for the first time—to present it in the form of slides as a keynote address at a symposium entitled "Transforming Visions: The Religious and Aesthetic in the Late-Twentieth Century," to be held in the Department of Religion at Syracuse University. Robert Thompson's stories about the appropriateness of context reflect my own fears. Will my mysticism be flagrantly out of place in this academic setting? Like Thompson's altar-makers, I welcome the chance to play with contrasting levels of reality, and to see just how vivid the self-made altar really is when you're explaining it to a room full of unsmiling professors. Several of the speakers have read my text in advance and prepared written responses, so I am anticipating some sort of challenge.

The moderator, Steve Leuthold, a suavely mannered professor of aesthetics, makes continual references to "Gablik's paper," a designation I can hardly get a handle on but which he can't seem to get enough of. But he does an excellent job of animating the scene with a volley of spray-paint questions, read from a loose-leaf binder, which get things going.

"I have to wonder about Gablik's implication that the magical and the mythological are more 'feminine' than masculine," he starts off, taking aim slowly. Then he pulls the trigger. "Her solution to the problem of patriarchy in religion—a problem that I do acknowledge—has been to turn to a gendered goddess, the Black Madonna. Does this compound the problem of gender in religion and spirituality, or help to solve it? Is thinking of God in gender-neutral terms as a kind of 'higher force' a better stance to take, or is this too depersonalized? Why should soul be felt to be feminine?"

As a good moderator, he has definitely started a few small fires. The jangled question of gender has rolled across my path before. In *The Reenchantment of Art*, I challenged the morally neutral, vision-centered paradigm of "patriarchal" aesthetics with more actively "feminine" values. I wondered then, and continue to wonder now, about the boomerang effect of using gender-based words as markers. Mostly it feeds on the polarity that is already entrenched in our language and our thought, and reinforces it. What if, like placing diamonds on a velvet cloth, we could introduce the perfect word for these so-called "feminine" values into the field of the world's awareness, would that change anything? Would it help us to become more receptive to this feeling-toned relational energy—instead of arguing indignantly and then turning the matter into a gender war?

As it turns out, Leuthold has even bigger game in mind than gender. For him, the whole matter of defining a personal altar as art seems to privatize, and perhaps even to compromise, what was once (and in his view still remains) a collective expression. How can we ever verify the spiritual authenticity of a personal altar? Although he is far too polite to confront me directly, I sense he feels there must be something bogus about a non-Catholic praying to the Black Madonna—and even worse, a Madonna boisterously decorated with a Native American spirit-catcher, a Celtic deity, and a reproduction of Lord Krishna. How seriously should one take this "intercultural," improvisational approach to spirituality? At what point does it all become like chop suey?

I am the first to admit to the composite, collage-like character of both my altar and my spiritual propensities—an exuberant eclecticism perfectly suited to an untenured, free-lance mystic like myself. But it is obvious that Leuthold is uncomfortable with what he perceives as a grab bag of unintegrated bits, pilfered from different traditions and then pieced together in some polysyllabic whole that, as far as he is concerned, doesn't quite make sense. Missing their connection with a living ground, are these objects, he wonders, merely echoing the forms of collective belief without their substance?

"Hell, no!" I want to yell back at him. "I got my mojo workin'."

Instead, I trade grinding a spiritual ax for good academic behavior. Doesn't he get it that for many people traditional religious institutions no longer work? Then comes the veiled reproach. "One must beware," he adds, "of inventing one's own myths or rituals, if they involve appropriation of key symbols from other cultures that have been radically decontextualized."

There's that word again! Picasso was criticized for the same sin when he appropriated specimens of African sculpture in his painting *Les Demoiselles d'Avignon*. It may have seemed like too much license at the time, but we, who now have all the hindsight, know that this shameless decontextualizing led to the birth of Cubism.

In his book on Marcel Duchamp, the Mexican writer Octavio Paz points out that ever since the breakdown of religion and metaphysics, our only idea, in the proper sense of the term, is criticism. It is, of course, the stock-in-trade of the university, the pillar holding it upright. In the end, although I find Leuthold's questions provocative and challenging, I do not share his epistemological panics. My interest in the Black Madonna as spiritual muse is less as a theologian or historian and more as a disciple: she just reached out and grabbed my heart. The Black Madonna provides the container into which my spiritual life can flow. Something deep down in me glimmers when I stare at her, awaiting revelation.

Six

AGENTS of inspiration arrive in one's life in many guises, often acting as a summons, alerting the soul to a prophetic journey of some kind. For author Sue Bender, it was the image of a begging bowl. The image simply erupted from her unconscious one day and arrived together with the words "Everyday Sacred." What had arrived was both an inspired icon, and a title for her next book. "All I knew about a begging bowl," Bender writes, "was that each day a monk goes out with the empty bowl in his hands. Whatever is placed in the bowl will be his nourishment for the day." Bender's book consists of the stories, people, and experiences that come to fill her bowl.

As a conjure object, the begging bowl is striking, because of its relaxed openness to the flow of life. One feels gratitude for whatever is placed in the bowl. I am conscious, as I read Bender's book, that her icon of emptiness and receptivity has no gender. There is nothing to dicker about here.

Often something read in a book will unravel a dilemma or pulse with personal meaning for me. After the symposium in Syracuse, my sense of an altar as a living dialogue to be questioned, struggled with, patiently illuminated, and even periodically reinterpreted, has been sharpened. Leuthold's comments continue to lodge in my consciousness like unstrung beads until I find myself, some weeks later, ignited by someone else's story. It happens as I read *Creation's Heartbeat: Following the Reindeer Spirit*, about the exotic spiritual journey of a woman who was summoned by a dream to run for months in the Arctic tundra with a herd of pregnant reindeer.

Linda Schierse Leonard, a Jungian analyst, was drawn to take an extended leave of absence from her practice in order to spend time with nomadic reindeer people in the Siberian wilderness and to travel with migrating herds of caribou in Alaska. Her desire for sensuous contact and communion with the reindeer led her to an almost clairvoyant state of fusion. "Inwardly, I entered upon a spiritual quest that challenged me to look at myself and my life anew," she writes. The reindeer became Leonard's teacher in the mystical feminine spirit.

In the shamanic culture of the Arctic tundra, reindeer are messengers and guides from the spirit realm, antlered angels bringing a sense of wild otherness from which to draw inspiration. According to Leonard, affirming our human kinship with these gentle creatures can teach us tenderness, or "doe wisdom," as she calls it: a feminine energy that is ecstatic, yet resolute and tenacious enough to endure through the coldest and darkest times, while still retaining the qualities of vulnerability and gentleness.

The reindeer became Leonard's icon. Whenever she loses her balance, she takes refuge in the reindeer image, in which she finds solace and healing. She remembers the look in the Siberian elder's eyes when he told her that "If the reindeer perish, so will we."

Reading Leonard's book puts me under the reindeer's spell. For weeks I think about the "earthed" spirituality of the reindeer. It too seems to incarnate something sheared clean of the gender trap. If I were to combine windswept reindeer with a "civilized" Madonna, the shamanic influence would rid my altar of its human, anthropomorphic bias as well. But how would I ever find a reindeer?

The reindeer finds me. I visit a new friend, the Reverend Chris Faulconer, who is an ordained minister, storyteller, shamanic counselor, healer, and ceremonialist. I hardly knew this woman when she told me she had been guided to come to Blacksburg by a voice emanating from the mountains, as she drove to visit friends one day, who live in the area. Chris followed the guidance, but now that she is here, she has discovered it is difficult earning enough money to stay. So she is planning to leave again, in the next few months.

As I walk through the front door of her apartment, I immediately set eyes on the reindeer: an anthracene blue-black stag, made of bronze. It is poised in midair on a shelf, flaunting its agility, its soaring antlers bearing two green candles. The sight of it turns me inside out, as if I'd just seen the Hope Diamond. Surrounding the reindeer is Chris's collection of Madonnas.

Even before we are comfortably installed on the sofa to chat over a cup of tea—and hardly aware of what I am doing—I ask if I can have the reindeer. Chris looks startled. I offer to replace the reindeer with a carved wooden Madonna that stands on a shelf in my bathroom. It would be a fair trade, I assure her, since the Madonna is quite beautiful and would fit in perfectly with the others she has. Already I am imagining the wild, sleek reindeer bedding down on my altar.

Chris stares at me, as if unaccustomed to such shocking presumption. I decide not to press it. At some point I tell her how the symbolism from Leonard's book has laid claim to my psyche. It turns out that Chris has read the book as well and also loved it.

Then, as I am leaving, abruptly and wordlessly, she hands me the reindeer. I feel my face light up, draw a full breath, and walk away gripping my new trophy.

Several days later, I return with the Madonna for Chris. In time, I learn that she has become an insatiable quester of Madonnas. Our ritual exchange of altar objects becomes the launching point for hearing a personal story that has many similarities with my own. It is the story, you might say, of the search for the lost feminine.

Chris grew up in California during the late 1940s and early '50s in a household that had no use for the church or for the feminine sensibility. At fourteen, without having even finished high school, she left home for good, determined to make it in the male-dominated world and support herself. But she recognized that in order to succeed in a world that was controlled by men, she would have to adopt a masculine persona.

After participating in the civil rights movement, protesting the Vietnam War, and becoming a feminist and political activist, she began to acknowledge the deep longing in her soul for something which, at that point, she could hardly even fathom. "I didn't have a name for it then," she said. "It was just an awareness that whatever it was I was looking for wasn't there."

Then, in her early forties, she found a teacher who was a psychic healer and who awakened her to the feminine principle of receptivity—without being submissive. "I became aware that my own feminine side had never developed, and that to come into balance, I needed that." But finding oneself exiled from one's gender is not a problem to be corrected overnight. It wasn't until she had a direct mystical experience that Chris understood, at an extremely deep level, what the meaning of all this was about.

She was traveling in a group of students with her teacher in Egypt. Early one morning, while visiting a Greek Orthodox church said to have been built over a grotto where Jesus and Mary once stopped to rest, Chris "dropped" spontaneously into an altered state and had a vision. She saw herself as a young peasant girl washing the feet of the Virgin Mary.

"What is the mystical faculty of perception?" asks Andrew Harvey. "Is it just a phosphorescent disease of the mind? Or is it actually a door opening on to the transcendent? Make up your mind, because what you decide will decide the whole of your life."

Chris was ready to deny what had happened, pass it off as a weird daydream. But another person, who had been sitting next to her in the church, said: "I saw you helping Mary in there." Chris realized that no matter how threatening the simple scene might be to her version of reality, it could not just be dismissed or denied. The sacred world had sprung full-bodied from this experience and was urging her to explore its significance. She decided to go with her vision.

"What I got out of it many months later was that I would serve her, in the way that I was serving her in that moment by washing her feet. It was clear that I would be doing the same thing in the later part of my life," she tells me. Now the Madonna personifies the ability to reach into, and gradually learn to live in, a state of patient receptivity. "It's the quality of compassion that I'm after. But of course I can't grab it, and I can't will it. I have to surrender into it. At the same time, I can't force myself to surrender; it's a question of sitting with it and of letting it influence me, and so of opening my heart in that way."

Andrew Harvey's visions were more frequent, and even more disorienting. But he made the same choice—not to dismiss them as whimsy or hallucinations, but to learn to follow their inner promptings. Harvey claims that mystical vision is everybody's destiny now, not a luxury for a few adepts—if we but have the courage to reach for it. In *Dialogues with a Modern Mystic*, he states: "Had I listened to the received wisdom of psychotherapy, I would have believed that all my visionary experience was psychotic. That would have set me back a lifetime."

Seven

THIS morning's mail unexpectedly brings an article about snakes, with an illustration of a juicy python. Clipped from *The Smithsonian*, it was sent to me by my best friend, Fern, who knows that my relationship with Tom is impregnated with the subtle energies of the snake. One of the things that attracts me to Tom is a fluid, undulating potency that can leap out, sudden and surprising, when you least expect it. Symbolically and mythologically the snake's reputation rests on an ability to shed its skin and arise renewed, implying the capacity for evolution.

One of the best days I ever spent with Tom was with Fern, when the three of us created the photographs for the cover of my book *Conversations Before the End of Time*. Fern had the idea of photographing Tom and me walking over a hill engrossed in conversation. Tom really unbuttoned himself for the occasion, bringing along his old Nikon and tripod from the days when he worked briefly as an army photographer. People who looked at the pictures later said they seemed to capture a mysterious etheric connection between us.

The minute I see the python, I think that it will make a perfect valentine for Tom. Some special truth about his deepest nature is intrinsic to this dramaturgy of the snake. Tom was born, according to the Chinese zodiac, in the year of the snake, and the essence of snake people is gathered strength, the quiet accumulation of energy in anticipation of the decisive moment. Snakes are reserved and secretive, keeping their emotions and ambitions well hidden, but they are also poor losers and take failure badly. They like to do things in their own way, in their own time.

Snake people are difficult to defeat once they are ready to move, but their chief weakness is sometimes to wait too long. I have to admit the snakelike pace is getting to me. Of course I've been warned, and have accepted the fact that this is going to take a long time. And I am learning a lot about the strength of self-direction and self-composure from the process. But I was also anxious to get things going.

I think I understand the problem, having read quite a bit about the male psyche in books like *Iron John* and *Fire in the Belly* which inspired the men's movement. I know about the four archetypes of the masculine personality that Jungian analysts Robert Moore and Douglas Gillette describe in *King, Warrior, Magician, Lover*. The Warrior archetype fits Tom to a T. The Warrior does not make his decisions out of emotional relatedness or personal feelings. He looks at his tasks unemotionally and acts out of transpersonal loyalty and honor. Though I can detect aspects of the King and the Magician in Tom's personality, the sense of connectedness and vulnerability of the Lover archetype seems to be missing. As far as I can tell, it has never unfurled. I've given Tom valentines before, and even on occasion sent letters stating my interest in being his partner, without much visible or clear response.

My first declaration of this kind was launched from Canada where I had gone to give some lectures. After I returned, Tom never referred directly to my letter. But he came for Thanksgiving dinner a few weeks later, bearing a large, succulent turkey that he cooked himself. When the other guests left, he stayed on, conversing jovially and sipping a little bit of wine as if in a symbolic toast with me. And then he left. It was a more blunted response than I had hoped for, but it hadn't felt like a rejection either. And sometimes, when I'm not expecting it, he gives me newspaper articles. If I study them with care, I can usually retrieve a secret charge of personal meaning attached to the text, rather the way that glimmer is to phosphorus.

The first time it happened, he gave me an article that described how dolphins inhabiting the Amazon River and its lakes have

SEVEN

become vulnerable and endangered, and badly need friends who can help in their preservation. The Ticuna Indians, who inhabit the region, believe that the dolphins have magical powers, and that they live much like humans, only underwater, attired in stingray hats and cuchafish shoes and wearing snakes for belts. In the lore of the Ticuna, finding a dolphin's tooth can bring good fortune, but stealing it can cause great harm to the thief. And if a human injures a dolphin, the dolphin will claim the spirit of that person as a punishment.

When I read the article, I immediately sensed that the vulnerable and endangered dolphins were a stand-in for Tom himself, who could be transgressed only at one's own peril. In Tom's world, there was no place for anyone who was predatory or disloyal. I also sensed that he was at a vulnerable time in his life and needed a friend.

Another article indicated a similar theme of rescue. A conservationist had designed a special, ultra-light, motorized glider plane, which he intended to use as a surrogate "Mother Goose" in order to entrain a flock of geese to fly along a more protected migratory route. To succeed, the pilot would have to fly slowly and steadily, never exceeding goose speed, so that the geese would be able to follow him while learning the new path. Again I found myself identifying with the turbocharged pilot and his idiosyncratic machine. And I sensed that Tom was trying to reprogram an unsatisfactory pattern in his life into another, more advantageous one. Of course I realize these interpretations may be overshooting the mark, but in my mind they shed light on what was happening.

Taking Fern's *Smithsonian* clipping, I cut out the python and paste it to a sheet of yellow paper. Then I insert the image of a tiny red rose into its mouth. I still need a message. I find a poem copied out in one of my notebooks which likens the creation of a whole person to the way that carbon crystallizes into diamonds after it has been buried long enough under the ground, and use that.

Now I had to decide about the heart-shaped cookie, which I'd taken from a huge jar on display for Valentine's Day in my favorite antique store, because of its message: BE MINE. "Bringing oneself to take the first step is a sign of inner clarity," the *I Ching* tells me. I wrap up the cookie in yellow tissue paper and put it into a small box. Everything feels like it is falling into place, yet fear is accumulating. I worry about receiving a rebuff. Tom is a fish for which you mustn't contrive a net. In Taoism, you do not force your way through obstacles. You understand that nothing is going to happen before its time and that at some point, without any strain, it simply slides through like silk.

The night before I am to deliver the valentine, the *I Ching* suddenly checkmates me, like some Machiavellian opponent. "Of its own accord," it says reprovingly, "the female principle comes to meet the male. It is an unfavorable and dangerous situation, and we must understand and promptly prevent the consequences."

Immediately I am on red alert. The warning rolls on. An inferior element has wormed its way in and must be energetically checked at once. I shouldn't underestimate its insignificance or seeming harmlessness.

The cookie! Its clichéd, preemptive message was willful—I see it right away. The *I Ching*'s description of a bold girl who of her own accord comes to meet the male and thus too lightly surrenders herself suddenly has a malignant ring that gives me a chill. I decide to deliver the snake valentine on its own and put the cookie, still in its box, into the altar drawer.

The oracle warns me to stay low and to be extremely cautious over the next few days—to make no attempt on my own to reach the desired end. "You are in a time when a transition must be made," it says, "but without going too far." If I am not extremely careful, it adds, somebody may come up from behind and strike me.

A day or so after I've sent the valentine, I see Tom drive by in his blue Mercedes. He gives me a transcendent wall-to-wall smile from behind the windscreen as his car passes mine. It's a wonderful smile, and I don't see it often, so it feels like a small benediction. But after that, there is no communication for several days. Except for the smile, my endearments seem to have fallen on thin air.

About a week later, he passes another newspaper clipping to me in class. I wait until I'm back home before daring to read it. As I scan the article, a few sentences scatter away from the rest and catch my eye. "... meticulous accuracy in one's statements is essential if one wishes to be heard." "We are at a critical point in agriculture when the people who purchase food must vote for their choices. It is time for some farmer/consumer interaction."

What's going on here? Vote for my choices? Time for some interaction? Have I understood the message? Was I being invited to go further in my overtures through these cryptic allusions to food distribution? Why on earth would Tom give me an article on agriculture and food distribution unless there was some concealed communication? It seemed absurd. I check again with the *I Ching*.

"The basic principle of any kind of union must be equally accessible to all concerned. Doubts and expectations need to be brought into the open, and goals realigned. Otherwise no progress can be made and nothing will come of the situation."

I get the cookie out of the drawer. And with the outboard motor running at full throttle, I write Tom a letter.

"If we are indeed at the point when we must vote for our choices, then here is mine. You, dear Tom, are my macaroni. It would make me very happy if I could be your cheese."

The letter goes on to praise his snaky ways, and his novel and exotic means of communicating through ordinary newspaper articles. "Talk about rabbits out of a hat," I wrote with neon-lit enthusiasm, "It's a class-A Houdini act."

Just to be sure—to get outside my own consciousness so I could see beyond it—I check guidance one more time for any hidden snags. The oracle positively undulates with encouragement. "Make hay while the sun shines," it says, "and tremendous progress can be made at this time. Assertive and confident contact will meet with a successful response."

I walk over to the altar. The Black Madonna sends off a rollicking smile. She seems to be observing me with amusement. I sense that I have just somersaulted into an unknown threshold in the saying of things, with no idea of what would happen next.

Eight

WHEN delicate desire sends forth its fragile vibrations in search of the true pole of magnetic rest in another human being, it must not be thwarted or there is devastation. So long as the force meets its polarized response all is well. But when a force flashes and has no response, there is devastation.

At our next class, Tom's response is sudden, swift, and lethal. "By the way, about those articles. They're just articles. They have no hidden meaning."

Suddenly it's as if the river I have been swimming in has been drained of water. Exposed and alone in the unforgiving landscape of cold, masculine consciousness, I feel as if I have just been boiled alive. And in a rush of unmastered feelings, I find myself wondering, perhaps for the first time, if Tom's heart is somewhere I could never reach. My Prince of Darkness has simply shrugged me off, the way a horse flicks away a fly, with a quick irreverent motion of its tail.

"How well the Tower defends itself!" declares the narrator in *Foucault's Pendulum*, the occult thriller by Umberto Eco. "From the distance it winks affectionately, but should you approach, should you attempt to penetrate the mystery, it will kill you, it will freeze your bones . . ."

Had I been stupid, then, or crazy, to interpret these articles as hidden communications? I had trusted implicitly that they were an entry point into the private universe of Tom's confidence. Should I have sacrificed the need to make my case and gone on waiting, without forcing or trying to grasp at what I wanted? Now it had become a dangerous game, in which my ego felt offended, tricked, blocked. I was sick with myself for sticking my neck out.

In disbelief, telling myself not to panic, I back out of the snake's lair. "If one leaps where there are always arms to take one up," James Hillman has written, "there is no real leap."

Later that night, I throw my three coins again for an *I Ching* reading. "The lake is empty, dried up," it says. "When one has something to say, it is not believed."

I couldn't stop seeing my defeat. Even Jesus counseled his disciples to quit towns that did not receive them, not to waste time or energy dealing with the neutered or the half-hearted. But not the *I Ching*. It had advised me not to judge on externals but to persevere quietly past all the obstacles. Now it was urging me to hold my path in spite of insults, injuries, or injustices—and to remain mild and pure, preserving the soft luster of jade.

But I'm not feeling lustrous, mild, or pure. What I really want is to kick Tom in the pants. Fifty barefoot kicks in the behind struck sideways so as not to hurt my toes. A good archer, however, makes sure her stance is correct before letting fly the arrow. If she fails to hit the mark, she does not hold it against her victor. Instead she catalyzes the event inside herself, and neutralizes its force internally.

On my altar there is a small, round talismanic box containing the pit of a peach; it's the relic of a fruit that was given to me as a gift one afternoon by Tom when his enthusiasms were flying high.

After I told Fern about the gift of the peach, she immediately wanted to know what I was going to do with it. You can't just eat it, she told me. So I entrusted the pit to a little box, along with some other small but significant items, and the box became my designated love charm.

Now everything had changed. The peach pit was the enemy. It was freeze and kill.

A few days later I light candles and incense at the altar and begin my ritual. I pull a card from the Motherpeace Tarot deck of a naked woman, standing in the Yogic Stork pose. She holds a white fea-

EIGHT

ther in each hand and waves them above her head. "The Two of Swords," the card says, "represents an attempt to gain mental balance and peace. The mind wants to be still, to avoid dealing with whatever might be happening in the external world...This temporary withdrawal stills the mind and gives a person time to figure out what to do next."

But I already know what I am going to do. I ring my little bronze bell three times and pass sage smoke over the box. After that, as a way of leaving my emotional fingerprint on the moment, I spit into the box. At exactly 10:25 A.M. on this cold and blustery February morning, I set forth for that little stream, not far from my house, where the current is strong. There, kneeling on the embankment, I lower the box and drop it into the stream. Whatever glass-eating, snake-charming, fire-walking powers have lured me into this mess, I have decided to let go of everything.

The little box floats in the stream like a cork, and begins to drift away from me. Then, my pocket-sized cargo suddenly veers towards the far embankment, where it gets moored in the mud. I had been hoping to watch it sail out of sight, but it soon becomes clear that the box has gone as far as it is going to go, at least for now. Slowly I retrace my steps back along the winding path of the creek, with the water racing past me over the stones, creating rivulets and little waterfalls. How could I have misjudged someone else's intentions so completely?

"Never *expect* things to work," writes Lyall Watson in *The Nature of Things*. "You must pretend that you don't care about the result. If pride or ambition is allowed to supervene, then a previously robust and accurate assay will suddenly fail. Nobody will ever discover the reason why."

At home, I sit again at the altar to bring closure to my ritual with one more Tarot card. This time, it's the Five of Swords, a five-pointed star composed of crossed swords on a yellow background, and a wasp arranged like a perfect photograph in the center of the star. "The Five of Swords represents a powerful negative experience, such as a defeat," it says. "The wasp in the center of the pentagram signifies a 'sting,' or some kind of focused pain. The downward pointing pentagram means the energy is being directed not as a blessing or protection, or even as a banishing spell, but as a hex or curse." The text continues to toll its cautionary message. Its promptings are unlike anything I might have expected.

The card continues, "The feeling of this card is something like, 'Damn you!' or 'I hate you!' Depending on the force behind it, the exclamation may or may not strike its victim in a conscious way. But it will certainly have repercussions on the psychic level." Clearly this isn't praise or support; it's a sobering reprimand. I now wonder if I did the right thing. The oracular reproach has flushed to the surface a great wave of resentments—towards Tom and towards the Black Madonna for bringing me down by a single blow.

"In this case" (the oracle hasn't finished with me yet), "a creative person might ask: 'Do I expect to get stung? Am I sure there has to be a winner and a loser to this? Am I willing to be cruel to get my way?' Inspired by the bright yellow mental energy surrounding the cursing pentagram, the personality may change her approach to the situation and give up power-tripping, anger and victimization."

Why didn't I see it? Killer energy had accompanied my dropping of that box into the stream. Spitting into the box had not been a good thing to do. Spitting has blasphemous connotations. It's like urinating on the crucifix. "Whenever I pronounce the word *civilization*," Gauguin once said, "I spit." The whole event was beginning to chill me.

Later that afternoon I drive home after eating a soothing bowl of soup in a restaurant. Something in my dark, cold, emotional landscape has changed. I can see that I need to return to the stream and—if it is still there in the wet leaves—retrieve my box.

This time the walk along the creek bed holds for me an odd blend of pleasure and terror in my jitteriness about whether or not the box will still be there. And then, in a moment of naked melodrama, as pure as any I have ever known, I see the box, still caught in the cleft of embankment where it had landed when I left. The sight makes me instantly buoyant and giddy. Is the explanation for this pure chance? A matter of water mechanics? Or is something more mysterious pointing me in a direction I haven't consciously chosen?

A few seconds of reconnoiter shows me that the only way I can reach the box is by fording the stream. I pick up a broken tree limb to use as support, and, still wearing my shoes and socks, slide my feet into the squishy bottom. In less than a minute I am across and able to grab the box. It has filled up with silty water, but the peach pit, my paper prayers, and the broken butterfly's wing are still intact. Perhaps it is an illusion, but I sense that the water has soothed and purified the contents and washed the injury away.

Gently I drain the water from the soggy box. Like a child who has just received an infusion of grace, I return my roving love trophy to its sanctuary on the altar. Now exhilarated, I feel as if I have been made the custodian of a magical secret: the beloved box I rejected has come back to me. Instead of weakening, my love object has been consecrated and empowered. "There are only two ways to live your life," Einstein once said. "One is as though nothing is a miracle. The other is as though everything is."

I close the ritual, one more time, with another Tarot card. This time the image is of two naked aboriginal women. The older one twirls the stick between her palms against another stick that is lying on the ground. She is showing the other one how to make fire —the means of getting what we want. Smoke emanates from the point where the two sticks meet. But it is the message, once again, that feels almost mediumistically accurate.

"The Two of Wands signifies the harnessing of one's personal power. The receiving part of the personality is open to learning; she watches and listens carefully as the older spirit shows her how to create the fire by friction." Many times during the ritual, it had seemed as though one portion of my mind were instructing the rest of me, as if something other than myself was showering me with insight. "Oracles do not only guide and inform us," writes Dianne Skafte in *Listening to the Oracle*, "they demonstrate that we are not alone in the universe."

Often in myths and fairy tales, when mistakes are made, it is clear that but for the mistake there would not have been a good outcome. The step beyond surrender is often magic. Without the emotional experiences of that afternoon, I might never have understood this amazing principle. That night, when I throw the *I Ching* before going to bed, my hexagram states that if we truly possess a thing it cannot be lost or destroyed.

We do not live the story, the story lives us. And the story will have its way.

Nine

"I AM ASTONISHED by how much I miss my altars I hadn't realized how important they had become," Paulus writes me from Tasmania, where he has gone to live for a year. He is staying in a tiny workman's hut at the edge of a lagoon with no heat, plumbing, electricity, or neighbors. Though Paulus is finding it a bit hard to manage in this self-imposed exile, he is learning new ways of sensing and experiencing, taking the leap of faith that can lead to a spiritual awakening.

"In the past," he writes, "when I would leave for any length of time and someone stayed in my home, I would ask them to light a candle on my main altar at least once a week. But this time, in order to make this trip, I had to give up my home, pack up and give away the things on my altars. I had hoped to build a 'proper altar' here, but I haven't had the heart yet. For a few days my altar was a tiny tree in a clearing, then a rock formation at the end of the beach—sandstone that had eroded into a Madonna. When I climb the four steps into this hut I feel as if I am climbing into the altar. Altar-consciousness enters my body—sometimes when I'm walking, I'm walking on the altar."

Altar-consciousness. I love the pleasurable drift of this phrase. It perfectly conveys the mulling and musing that are now my secret delight. In my case, however, altar-consciousness has come with a price I am not yet sure how to measure. I can see a whole new world has opened up to me that is aesthetically and spiritually satisfying, but at the same time I am losing my desire to do what I used to do: comment philosophically about issues of contemporary art in a form of prose that is detached, linear, and academic. It's as if my soul has made some sort of firm turn, and I can only communicate now from knowledge that is personal, experiential, and narrative.

More and more I notice that I am sliding around between two identities, shifting back and forth between two worlds. The sense that I've been overtaken by another identity comes over me when an invitation arrives to speak at an international conference of art critics in Reykjavik, Iceland.

Up until recently, I would have responded to such a proposal with a certain amount of excitement. Iceland, after all, is an intriguing place of almost no trees and black, volcanic beaches, a place where glaciers sit on top of volcanoes and rain can fall in any direction, even horizontally. The old me would have wanted to go without hesitation. As my correspondence with the conference organizers progresses, however, and they send suggestions for me to address, I become more and more reluctant to go. Questions such as: To whom does art criticism speak? Is it still possible to define an audience for art and art criticism, given the current forms of dissemination through the mass media? What are the political aspects of this system of dissemination for art criticism? Can art scenes flourish outside of this system?

Political aspects, mass media, systems of dissemination: the suggested topics for discussion pass me by like a stranger. Spread out on the table before me, the words fuse into an indistinguishable blur. They have no color, no weight, no liveliness. I am unable to produce answers to these questions. I don't think like this anymore. I decide I can't go: something in me has picked up and moved on. The complex bond that once secured and gave me my place in the world has become patchy at best, and rather like Alice when she fell into Wonderland, I have dropped through a deep hole only to find myself in another world.

Meanwhile, in my new world, I am stumbling badly, no longer where I used to be, but not where I am hoping to go either. As usual, I am waiting for a further development. As usual, there is none. The enigma of my situation with Tom remains unchanged. Despite the synchronicities of that afternoon at the stream, there is a deep pathos for me in the fact that the sacrificial moment had come and gone without, as my friend Fern liked to put it, anybody stepping up to the plate.

He has to step up to the plate, she'd say to me, on the phone from Chicago. Unless he steps up to the plate, you don't want him. I knew she was right. I was sick of hurling myself at a closed door. Certainly it was tempting to dismiss my situation as hopeless. And but for the experience of that afternoon at the stream, I would have.

I have to admit that whatever happened that day changed me, as if I had caught a glimpse of something a step or two beyond ordinary reality. Something really did seem to be collaborating with me and giving me instruction. I had felt myself being summoned across a swamp of fear and doubt. It was as though an invisible force was telling me everything was fine, all evidence to the contrary, and making sure I got glimpses of the larger picture so I wouldn't get bogged down in just one aspect of the story and give up. Meanwhile the *I Ching*'s counsel was more ominous and provocative than usual:

"You are in a position to realize your goal, but the sacrifices required are truly awesome. One must go through the water. It goes over one's head. Misfortune."

In walking the razor's edge, I was now developing an even more radical and rival quest to find out what, if anything, was encouraging me to continue on, even after I had already given up. For what had happened that afternoon at the stream—being guided to retrieve the box I had so deliberately tried to let go of—seemed to leave me with no choice but to try and find out. Because for me, another whole story begins right there: was someone or something really out there? "Does God stick a finger in, if only now and then?" Annie Dillard asks in *For the Time Being*. "Does God budge, nudge, hear, twitch, help? . . . Or is praying . . . for things and events, for rain and healing—delusional?" I needed to find out.

Contemporary culture is maintained by convincing us that nothing is out there. It is considered intellectually primitive to believe the world is infused with spiritual presences that are communicating with you and guiding you in some conscious, intelligent way. But what if this were wrong in some essential way? Still, I knew that some beliefs are held at the risk of catastrophe. Three hundred Plains Indians were killed at Wounded Knee while they were wearing their "ghost shirts," which they were convinced would protect them against the white man's bullets. And what about the Russian writer Gogol, who believed his stomach was upside down—and died of starvation? "In my solitude," the Spanish poet Antonio Machado once wrote, "I have seen things very clearly that were not true." If any clear-cut, embarrassingly naked human answers existed to these questions, they were what I was looking for.

A quest can take many forms. I had another reason for not giving up. Odd as it may seem, I had come to feel that I was living out a personal version of the Psyche-Eros myth. I began to use the myth like a plant taking in sunlight, as a graceful way of uncovering what to do next. I wanted to give up. Psyche never gives up. Confronted with a series of impossible tasks, Psyche receives magical help.
In the myth, Psyche doesn't know how Eros really looks, or even who he is. She has been forbidden to satisfy her curiosity about Eros by asking questions or by lighting the lamp. Eros will only appear to Psyche in the dark.
Inevitably Psyche's need to emerge from the darkness in which she is held captive impels her to transgress the taboo of Eros's invisibility. Egged on by her jealous sisters, she lights the lamp. But the price she must pay for this infringement brings ruin. Forced out into the open, Eros vanishes.
I knew from the myth that lighting the lamp makes Eros disappear, and I was determined to avoid Psyche's mistake by restraining my curiosity. Now I saw that Psyche has to light the lamp—it could not have been otherwise. Psyche's absurd predicament had become the inevitable core of my own experience.
I saw that I had been brought down, like Icarus, by my own

inflated exuberance. By interpreting the newspaper articles to Tom in a hyperbolic way, I realized I had stolen his secret and taken away the protective ring of his cover. Eros would rather muddy the waters than be revealed. His strength is in concealment. So all the little rituals and unconscious procedures which had made the process work and were impossible to replicate were best left to operate at unconscious levels.

When she loses Eros, Psyche doesn't make a fuss, doesn't respond with protest, defiance, or resistance. She simply accepts her fate. She doesn't struggle or attempt to escape her suffering; and she resists self-pity. Instead, she humbly goes about the tasks that have been created for her by Aphrodite, Eros's mother, who is jealous of Psyche's beauty.

The tasks prove impossible to fulfill. No heroic human effort can accomplish them. Before each task, Psyche falls into despair. The only solution seems to be to kill herself. But each time Psyche finds herself bereft of hope and immobilized by her condition, magic helpers from the plant and animal world come to the rescue, assist her in overcoming the obstacle, and set her on the right road again.

Psyche's most famous task is to sort out a hopeless muddle of seeds—a huge mound of barley, millet, poppy seeds, peas, lentils, and beans—into neat and tidy uniform piles, before morning. Only with the arrival of worker ants who help her can she do it. A magical intercession undoes the rope around her neck.

Somehow I have a feeling that my own fate parallels Psyche's. But then again, I'm not quite sure what Psyche's fate is. I don't really know, for instance, if Eros ever returns. After Psyche completes her journey to the underworld, does Eros come back? If the myth is going to be my talisman, I decide I'd better double-check the ending.

I make some interesting discoveries when I tackle Erich Neumann's commentaries in *Amor and Psyche*. The crux of the Psyche myth, according to Neumann, is that by her actions, Psyche creates her own redemption. She meets every situation inside herself, through developing her own inner powers. Without forcing the issue or taking any action, Psyche becomes by degrees stronger and stronger in her feminine self, and thus equal to the overpowering masculine force and able to endure its assault. But she never harms the masculine in any way. The feminine manner of defeating the dragon is to accept it.

And Eros does come back. Because of Psyche's courage and devotion, Eros is transformed from a burned fugitive and wounded boy into a man and savior. Neumann stresses again and again that Psyche's behavior is always "feminine"—she doesn't try to fix, change, or solve anything—and that the transformation of Eros is attained not by the efforts of Eros himself, but by Psyche's acts and sufferings. During her "extreme journey" of initiation, she acquires a "far-seeing" consciousness, and exorcises her own fear of what is to come.

The sublime ending of the story, according to Neumann, is the direct result of Psyche being true to herself and her love—a love which, for everyone else, is seen as an absurdity and an impossibility. But the true secret of it is observed by Psyche, even in opposition to Eros himself, and his passive and resisting masculine ego. Psyche has no regrets. She isn't afraid of dropping the ball, losing the deal, or failing the test. And that is what I like about her.

Ten

WHENEVER I identify myself with Psyche, my situation seems clearer, brighter, sharper. I have a sense of floating and a great calmness: my knowledge of the happy ending is a secret promise, drawing me like a magnet. And whenever a little "assisting miracle" comes my way, I feel an irrational belief that all will be well. But when I join the reality of my situation in the solid sensible world, it feels as if I am carrying on a losing battle, and all my uncertainties revive. I'm afraid of believing in things that aren't true.

In a world swaddled in skepticism, it is easy to lose the firm belief that one's intuitions are really going to lead somewhere. Holding the vision is proving to be a much harder job than I expected. But I also know it is part of the test. These contradictory pulls between faith and doubt are now at war within my being, and their shifting velocities had me at their mercies.

In the middle of one of these cycles of confusion and gloom, I find myself face to face on a sofa with John-Michael Dumais, an earnest, note-taking, psychospiritual therapist with a ponytail whom I met when he was conducting a "Celestine Prophecy" workshop in Blacksburg about a year ago. The workshop eventually mutated into a small group of people who got together for a while twice a month at his place. We called ourselves the "rimwalkers," a term meant to signify a willingness to push our lives more out on the edge. The great thing about John-Michael (besides his ponytail) is that he is perfectly at home with the crazy-making battle between my two minds—my struggle between doubt and trust.

After fixing me a cup of licorice tea, John-Michael asks me to do an exercise. He wants me to describe how I would feel if things were to work out with Tom. Taking the exercise to heart, I concentrate on trying to make these feelings conscious, vaguely aware that he is writing down my words on a piece of lined, yellow paper.

When I'm done, he hands me the list. A little embarrassed, I begin reading: "ecstatic joy; relief; the validation of my guidance and of the existence of magic; an affirmation of what is possible if one stays steadfast, in trust, however unlikely the Gestalt." At this moment, none of it seems realistic, which is why I'm here.

In an entirely even tone, John-Michael suggests that I accept fully in my consciousness that all of this is coming to me. Confidently he states that I should accept it is my destiny to experience these things, no matter what. I look at him as if this is the most ludicrous thing I've ever heard.

I'm ready for some kind of magic, I admit, but the idea that a visualization swaggering with hope and expectation is going to get me what I want makes me recoil. I feel more at home chained to my rock of doubt in the wilderness.

Undaunted, John-Michael is ready with another exercise. "Imagine yourself sitting on the back deck of your house." With a few gentle breaths, he drifts me there, as on a zephyr. Then he says: "The door opens and a Black Madonna appears. Now tell me what is happening."

Creative visualization is not something I practice. I've been slow to warm up to this popular New Age technique, and am not very good at it. But this time I see a figure coming towards me, moving briskly. She wears a jet-black dress made of stiffened taffeta, with strange perpendicular ruffles everywhere. Her arms are outstretched as if about to greet a long-lost friend. We embrace, but instead of pulling back from me, some invisible suction causes the Black Madonna to vanish into my solar plexus. And in that merging, that fusion, it feels as if her rich essence, her magic or whatever it is, enters directly into me.

TEN

From the minute I feel penetrated by the Black Madonna, it's as if I have experienced a call of some kind, a spiritual beckoning. Suddenly I know exactly what I am supposed to do.

That night I telephone my friend Lorna Roberts in New York and sign on for a pilgrimage journey she is leading, to visit sanctuaries of the Black Madonna in the great basilicas of France. I sense that I am being called to undertake the "dark work" of communion, to make my relationship with the Black Madonna more conscious, by entering directly into her charged field. Spiritual pilgrimage is something that is often undertaken at a critical juncture in one's life. I am not exactly sure what it is that I am looking for: some unexpected illumination, or my very own "burning bush" adventure. Perhaps, if I listen quietly in the dark silent tabernacles, the Black Madonna will speak to me. Amid the flicker of candles, perhaps I will even touch her, if I can.

Eleven

WE are eight women, badly crumpled from the all-night journey on Air France, headed out in a rented gray minivan from Charles de Gaulle airport towards our first Black Madonna in central France. Most of us have been traveling pretty non-stop for two days from different states in the U.S., and the atmosphere in the van is a combustible combination of exhaustion and elation. Our transit is not over; there are still five more hours of driving before we get to the hotel in Royat, a small town in the Clermont-Ferrand region, where we will spend the night.

Our first adventure occurs within minutes of taking off in the van, when a wrong turn puts us, not on the exit road from the airport, but on an entry ramp spiraling down ever more deeply into an underground carport. Before we know it we are enmeshed, unable to drive the van inside because of the low ceiling that will snag the roof rack if we try to go under it, and unable to maneuver the van backwards up the ramp either, because of the steady stream of French drivers hurtling down at breakneck speed with no time to lose.

The ramp quickly becomes an aquarium filled with exhaust fumes and irate drivers. It takes several complicated procedures and more than an hour before we are finally released from our strange plunge into the underworld and launched correctly onto the highway out of town.

Eventually we are winding gracefully past fields of emerald green grass and golden expanses of flowering mustard plants. The city has been left behind, but we are still three-hundred kilometers from our destination and won't arrive before dark. Everyone is looking forward to a delectable French dinner, a glass of wine, and most especially, a bed.

Hours later we finally reach the small town of Royat just before a storm breaks. The sky becomes spectral, blackening with incredible rapidity. All of a sudden, smoke rises up visibly from under the hood of the van. Everyone winces with dismay, as one by one we stagger out onto the sidewalk in the darkness, to assess what new disaster is now overthrowing any hope of refuge. But the disaster folds back on itself just as quickly as it started when it is discovered that our hotel is only a few yards up the street, and relief is at hand. The proprietor greets us like beloved friends. We are the only guests. The van can be repaired in the morning, and there is a genial restaurant nearby. In great happiness, I fall upon the curling salad greens and warm goat cheese; and finally, overwhelmed with fatigue and good wine, my whole body quietly subsides into buttery cotton sheets.

The next morning in the hotel I try to prepare myself for my first encounter with a Black Madonna. What will she be like? Am I going to fall in love with her? Is she really a divine presence? Finally we enter the church of Notre-Dame du Marthuret in Riom, the town next to Royat. Here I am at last, in the presence of the sought-for symbol, staring into eyes that immediately engage mine. Her soft smile flickers as quietly as the Mona Lisa's. She is perfect, beautiful without a fault, mysterious and exciting. We seem to understand each other, and now that I see her, I can tell clearly that her blackness is not the result of any accretion of candle smoke, but the potent intention of a possessed craftsman, who set about his task over days and nights of effort.

She is garbed in a sapphire-blue cloak—painted with tiny *fleurs-de-lys*, the symbol, since Merovingian, times, of the French royal family—which is wrapped around her shoulders on top of a vermilion red dress. She reminds me of Black Isis, the Egyptian goddess who wears a robe bedecked with stars. The extended right hand is open and beckoning. Sitting jauntily on her left knee is the Child, dressed in a robe the color of pea soup. On one side of the gold pedestal a candle burns brightly in a crimson glass holder, and on the other side, someone has put a vase of purple irises, like an offering prayer.

Silently, our little band of pilgrims gathers in the pew benches facing the Madonna to pay tribute. The group is harmonious and homogeneous—modest, low-keyed, soft-spoken women, bound together by an eaglelike alertness and inquisitiveness about the Black Madonna. We have all come to practice reverence and to develop what the visionary priest Matthew Fox calls "muscles of receptivity." Two of the women are teachers from the Midwest, working in Women's Studies; two are in computer-related businesses in Minneapolis and Santa Fe; one is an artist from Maryland, with long gray braids, who acts as Lorna's assistant. But the jewel in the crown of our journey turns out to be Lorna's mother Gladys, in all the glory of her eighty-four years and richly endowed with crone wisdom and equanimity.

No one in our group, it turns out, practices traditional Catholic worship. Yet there is a common sympathy for the Black Madonna as an independent "postdenominational" source of sacred power that is individualized rather than formulaic, experiential rather than doctrinaire. As a symbol, she seems to capture the way that the scientific world view and masculine mind is being reconfigured in the contemporary psyche, personifying the search for soul at a time when impersonal soullessness no longer seems appropriate to our changing culture.

An intense sense of shock pervades these first moments of contact with the Black Madonna, powerful feelings that cannot be expressed easily but perhaps resemble all that D. H. Lawrence felt when he first encountered American Indian culture. "I shall never forget that first evening when I first came into contact with Red Men, away in the Apache country," he wrote in an essay. "It was not what I had thought it would be. It was something of a shock. Again something in my soul broke down, letting in a bitterer dark, a pungent awakening to the lost past, old darkness, new terror, new root-griefs, old root-richnesses."

She is keenly watched and keenly felt by all these women whose presence here is the climax of many infinitesimal steps and decisions to fertilize their spirits and embrace the feminine aspect of themselves. In some sense we are all here to reframe the old myth—that of the God of patriarchal religions, who is never seen as being in creative partnership with a Goddess, and to take action to make a new story come true. We are here, in postures and attitudes of reverence, to discover a new solar system in the making, whose central sun is not ordinary cognition but trust in the alchemical darkness.

That evening, it pours with rain again. We dine convivially in a charming brasserie, while the prospect, at least to me, of a night-time procession in the town of Marsat in the rain looms somewhat distastefully on the immediate horizon. Nevertheless, we are traveling in the energy field of the Black Madonna, and we are on pilgrimage, which means forging ahead into darkness and no slinking back into comfort. Tonight the Madonna will be taken outside and carried through the streets on a throne, floating in air against the night sky as we walk, along with hundreds of others, behind her.

Murmuring sounds of choral music infuse the atmosphere as we enter the church. Miraculously, the rain stops just in time for the ritual. In the vestibule, two women sell long white tapers and paper lanterns at a table. We stop to buy some to hold while we walk; the glow from the candles can be seen for miles around, tiny clusters of light gleaming in the darkness.

Inside the church, melancholic priests intone the liturgy in French, ritually thanking the Mother for the gift of her Son. I am startled by the willful phrasing of the words, realizing that even on this, her own festival day, the Black Madonna is not being acknowledged as an object of reverence in her own right, but enjoys this special moment of veneration only in her auxiliary role as the mother of a male God. He is the real source of creativity and generativity; she is the facilitator. That would make her Mary, except that she is as black as the ace of spades. We may only guess at the real mystery of her origins, which goes undeciphered and unacknowledged.

I watch in fascination as the priests attach gold crowns to the heads of the Madonna and Child. This Black Madonna is almost tersely beautiful, sphinxlike even, her gaunt, aristocratic, obsidian face framed by a gilt cowl that descends in sinuous, circular sweeps across her body, covering everything except her extremely large hands, strong and bony, which represent healing energies and spiritual regeneration. Inevitably I sense the undercurrents of her pagan past, the fusing and blending of Eastern and Western traditions, an amalgam of Egyptian, Babylonian, Greek, Islamic, and Jewish influences: the coming together of the world religions. The Black Madonna is not unique to Christianity.

As the priests lift her into the four-columned, open-sided pergola, I am struck by how perfunctory and disinterested, and without emotion, their movements are. It is a curious, expressionless tableau, as if they are handling a gunny sack of potatoes. From their stiffly held necks and averted gazes, I realize how much the archetypal power of the Black Madonna has the whole weight of priestly privilege and authority against it.

As far as I can tell, there is a tremendous difference between the modest prestige of the Black Madonna today and the mystic feelings that surrounded her as the adored ideal of heretical cults during the Middle Ages, which included the troubadour culture of Provence, the Cathars and the Knights Templar. When they first appeared in France, Black Virgins were linked with a path of initiation, associated with esoteric Mystery Schools, in which initiates learned about the hidden powers of human consciousness by submitting to a renunciation of their individuality, and surrendering up the need to be in control (a symbolic shift from masculine to feminine). Often the placement of Black Virgins in grottoes and underground crypts—or, as in the case of Chartres, next to a well with healing waters—signaled their connection with the regenerating powers of earth. Black Virgins also figure prominently on the nearly five-hundred-mile great pilgrimage route, the Camino of

Santiago de Compostela, that begins in France, crosses the Pyrenees, and runs from east to west across northern Spain until it reaches the cathedral of Santiago de Compostela.

Hoisting the pergola up onto their shoulders, four men in business suits carry the Madonna outside, where a young boy who wears an iron cross and two small girls dressed in crisp, white dresses and holding lanterns, wait to lead the procession. I link arms with one of the other women in our group, and we plant ourselves directly behind the holy idol, in one of the front rows. Clasping our lit candles, we begin to move as one body, silent and intent, through the slanting streets of the town. The walk in the darkness is intoxicating, almost like a sensuous drug. While everyone prays and chants, the sound is magnified dramatically by microphones and acoustic systems that are carried alongside us. The dreamlike mood is interrupted several times when the flame from one or the other of our tapers glimmers out. Once I lean over to try and reignite my candle carefully from my companion's, without breaking the rhythm of our walking. As our two hands twitch nervously in the air for a few seconds, and both candles go out for good, I have to stifle an anarchic urge to giggle uncontrollably.

For the rest of the hour we walk with no lights until, having looped through the village, we are back in the courtyard of the church, our solemn progress ended.

During the next few days, we encounter several more Black Madonnas, in churches at Clermont-Ferrand, Le Puy-en-Velay, and Besse, but it is at La Chapelle Geneste, in the stillness of an empty chapel far away from any big town, that we happen on the supreme icon. This Madonna is seated at the back of the chapel, in a niche which has been painted a faded, powdery, sea-colored blue. Wreathed above her head are four cherubim holding a crown. Her face is like an obsidian fragment; from her coal-black face brilliant sky blue eyes look straight out. Painted blood-red, her ripe mouth exudes an enigmatic charm. Slung over her strong body is a golden robe, gleaming like honey. The dense, fierce blackness and hieratic frontal posture remind me again of Isis and her son Horus, whose iconography was adopted by Christians to portray Mary and Jesus. How easy to see her as the Creation, the very core and center to the world—a wick palpably soaking up souls. This striking black chunk of beauty sweeps away any lingering presumption that the divine must be white, male, and bearded.

By virtue of this proximity, it seems clear that the Black Madonna is truly our next great adventure, the icon of a mystic renaissance in our culture. She is, as Andrew Harvey suggests, the herald of a social transformation that is a pressing necessity—our civilization's next enterprise—without which we cannot, in fact, go forward. The Black Madonna is our fall into the future.

Twelve

IF THERE is a dark heart to our journey, I suppose it is the unseen presence of Mary Magdalene, whose story, from our present vantage point, can only be guessed at. Still scrabbling over the face of France in our own sweet time, traveling south from the Auvergne through rocky, mountainous country, we head towards Provence and the legendary cave of Ste. Baume, where Mary Magdalene is supposed to have spent the final thirty years of her life, shivering and praying, after she fled to France in the aftermath of the Crucifixion.

Who was Mary Magdalene? According to religious scholar Margaret Starbird, she is the "other Mary," scorned and repudiated by Christian theology, the "Lost Bride of the Canticles," Mary of Bethany, who was not Jesus' mother, but his Bride. This version of the Christian story is definitely not taught in established Christian churches. In "orthodox" depictions, Mary Magdalene is described as a prostitute who became a follower of Christ after being healed by Him, and by implication, giving up her sexuality. She is often pictured in Western art as a penitent prostitute bearing, at the foot of the Cross, an alabaster jar of precious ointment.

In her book *The Woman with the Alabaster Jar,* Margaret Starbird suggests there is strong evidence, found in the Coptic scrolls discovered in Egypt at Nag Hammadi in 1945, that Mary Magdalene was the center of a cult that flowered in Provence for centuries, and was worshipped in the Middle Ages by heretical sects including the Cathars, Knights Templar, and Albigensians, all of whom believed she was the Beloved of Jesus and that they had a child.

As consort, partner, and Beloved, Mary Magdalene is quite distinct from the Virgin Mary, who is worshipped as Jesus' Mother.

"Beautiful as this mother is," Starbird writes, "it is clear that someone very real and precious is missing from the Christian story." Starbird even goes so far as to suggest the possibility that the Black Madonnas of the early shrines in Europe (from the fifth to the twelfth centuries) might have been venerated as the symbol of this other "outcast" Mary and *her* child—who were brought to the coast of France thirteen years after the Crucifixion by the "other Joseph," Joseph of Arimathea.

This auspicious prospering and expansion of the feminine principle in Provence was ruthlessly suppressed by the Vatican during the Inquisition, at which time a crucial split occurred in Western culture between the maternal-spiritual and the erotic-sensual aspects of the feminine. Rejected out of fear, the cult of the Black Virgin was absorbed and conflated into the cult of the Virgin Mary. The hidden subtext of this conflation was intended to honor only the Mother and Sister aspects of the feminine. It excluded the Bride. Starbird asserts the suppressing came about when the Church of Rome perceived great danger in allowing the rumor of Jesus' marriage and alleged bloodline to circulate. The Roman Catholic Church moved quickly and firmly in the thirteenth century to ensure that it was the mother of Jesus, and not his wife, who was venerated.

"I know of no way to prove beyond a doubt that the 'other Mary' was the wife of Jesus or that she bore a child of his bloodline," Starbird writes. "But it *is* possible to prove that belief in this version of the Christian story was widespread in Europe during the Dark and Middle Ages and that it was later forced underground by the ruthless tortures of the Inquisition."

It is a bright, sunny morning as we set out for the cave. Many saints, including Catherine of Siena, have made the strenuous pilgrimage to this place in the past, as have—if one can believe the local tourist literature—all the kings of France. Getting there requires a trek though a forest of ancient oaks and beeches whose branches create a natural arch over the trail. The trek ends in a steep

TWELVE

climb of one hundred and fifty steps to the entrance of the cave.

The prospect of the cave excites me. Somewhere in the back of my mind, it has become for me a pinnacle of the journey, this sanctuary in the heart of the forest where Mary Magdalene accomplished her great withdrawal, separating herself like a sylvan divinity from the rest of the world. Improbable as it may seem, I am hoping for some revelation or message here—perhaps another consecration of some kind. For this reason, I have brought along the little votive box, which I rescued from the stream in Virginia. It is stuffed into the pocket of my shorts.

When the others decide to pause at the end of our hike in order to perform a small ceremony as a preparation for entering the cave, I decide, on my own selfish tack, to forge up the last remaining bit of the trail by myself, so I can arrive at the cave ahead of everyone else. I will need time to take in the atmosphere, to inhale the fumes radiating from cracks in the earth, to merge into the darkness so I can understand what I am to do here. I realize that the thought carries a pinprick of anxiety.

The entrance to the cave, I discover, is equipped with heavy wooden doors. The modern stained glass windows on one side of the cave are something of a disappointing surprise. A gigantic, ten-foot, triune Crucifixion is placed up against the naked living rock of the cave wall, giving the painful impression that three dead sentries are guarding the cave. When I step through the giant portico, I find myself inside the cave, alone.

The interior is unexpectedly large, riddled with humps and hollows, and cluttered with altars. There is a subdued sound of water dripping, and the darkness is illuminated by racks of blazing candles, whose tiny flames of yellow light are reflected upon the wet floor. A high altar featuring another crucified Christ fills the central space; rows of pew benches are neatly lined up in front of it. Set back under the natural cave wall, well behind the Christ, I find a gleaming white statue of Mary Magdalene being raised up by the angels. It is a cloying genre piece of the worst sort of nineteenth-century academicism. This version of Mary Magdalene is indistinguishable from representations of the Virgin Mary. Here is the conflation of the two Marys that Margaret Starbird talks about. This glacially white and cloying statue makes it difficult to imagine the real Mary Magdalene, bogged down in darkness and stooping under the rain, warming her frozen hands over a brazier. None of this feels artistically right.

According to one of my brochures, Mary Magdelene "took neither food nor material drink, but at each hour of prayer the angels descended from Heaven and raised her into the air and she heard the Heavenly choir and then she was descended into the cave hollowed out of the rock." The symbolic function of "white" Virgins, it seems, has always been to suggest that we take to the air—leave our bodies and go to some religious otherworld.

Off in another corner, where you can hardly see her, I discover a second figure of Mary Magdalene, also white and sculpted in the same academic mode. Yet this one has a real emotional presence. She crouches, and cradling a Cross in her arms as though it were a child, she looks small and tender and achingly lonely. Someone has left a votive candle at her feet and placed a bouquet of roses on her lap. I make an awkward bow. Then I run my hand along the cave wall behind her for a brief moment. The surface of the rock is damp and crumbling from the steady stream of water descending from a hidden source. It leaves a black, alluvial deposit on my fingers. I have a curious desire to scrape the precious granules into my box as an offering, standing on the wet floor, as if in the amniotic fluid of the earth.

Moments later, the rest of the group arrives. In the dim light they find places in which to do their meditations. A workman appears, and soon the hard clang of his hammering on the benches drives me out of the cave and into the blinding light. So far nothing really auspicious has happened. I still hold the small round cardboard box in the palm of my hand. Now any hope of inspiration seems to have been lost.

Then I notice a creeping vine that surrounds the entrance to the cave and spreads up the stout limestone cliff like a scintillating carpet. A velvet green leaf collected from this holy ground would be a tangible reminder of my time here. Quickly, I snare one and put it into my box, laying it like a healing poultice on top of the peach pit, where it fits perfectly.

  When I open the box a few days later, I discover that the leaf has migrated up to the lid, rising like a balloon and attaching itself there. The displacement strikes me as odd, but I do not think too much about it. A few days later, when I open the box again, I find that the leaf has now descended from the lid and nestled itself way down inside the box. It is lying side by side in what looks like a wild, sweet coupling with the peach pit.

  Mystical vision, seeing something extraordinary by way of the ordinary, does not necessarily happen when you are expecting it. But the gods will often speak through enigmatic messages, and the more we learn to listen, the more they speak to us. However farfetched this may seem to anyone else, I confess that in this unaccountable flicker of movement, I saw a repetition of the theme of separation and return which crosses the Psyche myth, and which was first transmitted to me through the box, and my experiences with it, that day at the stream. I felt as if I'd had a communication from the living intelligence of the cosmos, and that it had touched the deepest part of my being.

  "To the contemporary mind, the notion there might be messages or signs within random events seems strange, even absurd," Ray Grasse has written in *The Waking Dream*. "Yet for millennia, such perceptions were commonplace around the world. . . . As seen from this ancient perspective, reality is pregnant with hidden meanings and connections waiting to be unlocked by the discerning mind."

  The suggestion that life is a sacred text waiting to be unlocked through the key of metaphoric knowing is very attractive to me. Grasse maintains that much of what we consign to background noise in our lives may really be signal, or revelation. The passage of a bird through the sky, for instance, or the appearance of lightning at a critical moment, the overhearing of a chance remark, are all significant to the degree that they are perceived as interwoven within a greater tapestry of relationship and can thus be deciphered for their higher significance. Yet because we have forgotten the language of these symbols and how to read them—our personal hieroglyphics—this dimension of knowledge remains closed to us, even though it is actually at our fingertips.

This was my dilemma: I couldn't really tell if my mind was becoming more discerning in the language of symbols, or whether I was just delusional. But I was beginning to see that my attempt to live magically and symbolically in a culture-based rational and scientific explanation is a challenge that might put my whole being at risk. I had entered a bewildering twilight zone where it was impossible to know how trusting I should be.

Sensibly, could I dare, without surrendering into utter foolishness, to stake my future on the deviant wanderings of a migrant leaf? After all, according to James Hillman in *The Soul's Code*, "it's a bean that saves Jack, and a pebble that saves David from Goliath. Stupidity is the giant that misses the small things." If I silenced the critic, the skeptic, would I be setting out for some dim headland on a rotted log, in fast water? And would I end up, as my culture invites me to believe, sinking into a swamp of delusion, with my arms flailing?

I was once interviewed by a professor of religious studies, who was writing a book about "autonomous spiritual seekers"—people whose spiritual realizations come through direct experience rather than through dogmatic belief. She asked me: "Would you be disappointed if you found out the material world is all there is?"

Of course I would. The question strikes at the very heart of one's view of reality, and everything rides on the answer. In my own case, I prefer to think there is a secret staircase, hidden behind the waterfall, which all of us are climbing, whether we can see it or not.

Thirteen

ON THE EIGHTH DAY of our pilgrimage, we enter what looks just like a scene from a Jean Renoir movie: the brooding and reflective world of the Camargue, with its views of salt marshes, white horses, pink flamingoes, and drifting mist. We have come to attend the festival of the black Saint Sara, patron saint of the Romany gypsies in the town of Les Saintes-Maries-de-la-Mer. Sara, the Black Queen, is described in the *Everyman Dictionary of Non-Classical Mythology* as an extension of the cult of Isis, after Christianity took over her chapels and her images. An added commentary states that in Les Saintes-Maries-de-la-Mer, "Isis has been demoted to the rank of a serving maid with the name of Sara, in which capacity she is still the divinity of the gypsies." Sara is said to be the black Egyptian servant who accompanied Mary Magdalene and others to France, where they arrived from Palestine in a leaky boat without oars or sails.

Today, the seaport town of Les Saintes-Maries-de-la-Mer is a scene of incredible animation, swarming everywhere with gypsies. The women are dressed in outfits of brightly colored satin and lace, with sequined bodices and ruffled skirts, their dark insouciant sexuality vividly on display. The men are beautifully ostentatious as well, in gold lamé jackets and fringed vests and palpably tight hipster pants. Wherever I look, mariachi bands are playing, all around the great plaza, in cafés and restaurants, and even on the tessellated roof of the church, with much fierce handclapping accompanying the guitars. There is a quickness, an elegance and grace to it all, that makes me want to stay here forever.

I am settled down comfortably with Lorna and her mother in a café overlooking the church, while we wait for the doors to open, signaling that the procession to bring Sara down to the sea for immersion will begin.

Lorna and I wear identical khaki sunhats, acquired only moments ago in a tourist shop around the corner. As I sit quietly watching her from behind my cappuccino, I think how beautiful she looks, her sea-blue T-shirt setting off her sooty, blue-gray eyes. I feel grateful for this stroke of luck, being here with my friend in a French café, dissolved in the pleasure of participating in a seething pageant of gypsies and luminous colors and pounding guitars. From the serendipitous moment she turned up at a lecture I once gave at the New School for Social Research in New York and asked a question from the audience that radiated such radical free spirit, such electricity, I recognized a remarkable soul.

That night, after the lecture, we went to a café together and talked for hours. I learned she had been a painter, living with her husband and two children in a brownstone in Greenwich Village—the same house where the poet e.e. cummings had lived for years. Then shamanism became a feature of Lorna's life. She trained in the Peruvian lineage, eventually becoming initiated by her American teacher, Alberto Villoldo, and a jungle shaman, Agustin Rivas. During the process, however, her marriage became irrevocably unmoored; it was a stabbing loss that left great scars. After that, Lorna established Triquetra Journeys, a business in which, several times a year, she leads people on shamanic journeys to Peru—and more recently, to France to visit shrines of the Black Madonna.*

Finally the doors of the church open, and people begin streaming out. But they are not carrying Sara. For a moment we are tipped off balance. Where is she? Our shock would be hard to imagine when, upon further investigation, we discover that a wire has been crossed in our scheduling: the procession to the sea will not happen

---

*Regrettably, after a long bout with cancer, Lorna Roberts died in Kansas on the morning of September 11, 2001.

THIRTEEN

until tomorrow. We are due to leave later this afternoon.

Absorbed in the confusion of the moment, nearly faint with disappointment, we begin to push our way into the church, past the surging crowd of people who are coming out. We find Sara in the crypt downstairs, ringed by more hordes of gypsies straining to get close. Hundreds of candles are burning, emitting an almost convulsive heat. There are so many bristling, energized bodies focused on Sara that we couldn't escape, even if we wanted to.

There is no doubting the intensity of their love for her. She is the object of a complex ecstatic experience we rarely experience in our culture—which includes the possibility of dressing her up, pinning things on her, crying at her feet, even kissing her.

She is slightly less than life-size, but she seems almost lifelike, because of the tightly packed layers of clothing in which she is bundled. Her outer garment, a bright red satin cassock, is wreathed at the shoulders by a wide-aproned, glazed white collar made of lurex and spangled with black polka dots. It frames her poignant brown face, a rich cocoa color, in flutes of spun sugar, so that it seems to float, like a moon on water. There is a gold lurex scarf tied at her throat, above which is pinned a corsage of scarlet ribbons in the form of a heart.

I merge with the moving throng inching its way towards a moment of direct physical contact with the icon. In front of me, people are soaking up her sweetness. One man leans over and kisses her on the lips. Another holds her head lovingly in his hands and cradles it. I watch him soften with tenderness. Then it is my turn. Lightly I touch Sara's face, the length of dulcet cheek as alluring as putting your hand on a wild deer. And then, quickly, I try to capture her vision in a photo.

After a big lunch of paella and wine and serenades, we drive to Arles and spend the night in a small, saffron-colored hotel. From there, in the morning we set out on our most arduous trek so far, as we leave the Camargue and travel west into the Languedoc in search of a thirteenth-century chateau called Castlefranc, which is located in an obscure segment of countryside known as Montredon Labessonie, in the Tarn area of southwest France. We have received special permission to do a shamanic fire ceremony here. Lorna, who believes that the Gnostic tradition of the Black Madonna resonates in fascinating ways with shamanism, likes to combine them in a ritual experience. "You're not just given a dogma in which you either believe it or else go to hell," she says, of both traditions. "You come to gnosis (inner knowing) through direct experience, and that is utterly shamanic."

Chateau Castelfranc proves difficult to find, and our normally easy-going troupe becomes enervated when we realize that we have been driving around in circles for some time. Finally, exhausted and bedraggled, we pull into a gravel driveway deep in the woods and fall out of the van like "drugged squirrels," as the joke of the moment has it. We are greeted by the welcoming smile and waving arms of George, a solid and imposing Englishman, who turns out to be the manager-caretaker of the place.

Our abode for the next two nights is a thirty-room, ancient, thirteenth-century chateau, with its own chapel and cloister. It has been recently bought and put under restoration by the Dandelion Trust, an English charity dedicated to saving land and buildings. Castelfranc has just begun its life as a conference and retreat center—we are the second group to stay there. It seems that the chateau's original owner was a Cathar, who was routed out during the Inquisition under charges of heresy and then killed. In another time, unspeakable acts must have happened here.

We are directed to our rooms by George, who explains that there are no keys. Mine is upstairs, a kind of monk's cell with nothing in it except a bed and a window. When I wake up the next morning, all I can see are the cold fog and drizzle that have swallowed up the world outside.

Winds roll in, rippling through the forest. Not good weather conditions for a fire ceremony. Several people have developed colds. We decide to shift the proceedings inside, rather than gather on wet ground. George balks at our request to use the fireplace in the living room, concerned that the drumming and chanting will disturb the sleep of his visiting grandchildren. Instead, he settles for something wonderful. He agrees to open up the abandoned chapel and let us use it for our ceremony. We won't be able to make a fire in the chapel, however, but will have to confine ourselves to lighting candles.

What is the purpose of holding a shamanic fire ceremony from the tradition of the Peruvian jungle in the middle of a forest in France? According to Lorna, it serves as a stimulus for quickening one's own healing and development in a moment of pure concentration and prayer. We will also use the experience of ritual as a means of communing with the energies of the Black Madonna. Fire ceremonies of this kind involve individuals working privately and silently, one by one at the fire, focusing their intention around some special issue in their life that is to be either "released" or "invited in." Each person is instructed to bring with them, if they wish, an object or possession, or perhaps something they have made, which can be offered to the fire as food for the flames. Then, supported by the shaman's presence, the individual passes her hands through the fire, drawing its energy and heat into the energy centers of the body, beginning with the belly, then the heart, the third eye, and finally, the crown of the head.

That afternoon, improvising with objects brought from the chateau, we begin to transform, slowly and rhapsodically, the damp, musty, falling-to-ruins chapel with our fresh harvest of altars. On the left-hand wall is a trio of conveniently empty niches, left over from some remoter moment in history when they were filled with religious statuary before being looted by thieves. The niches make a perfect setting for our own carefully chosen votive objects: the miniature replicas of the Black Madonna we found in Le Puy, their tiny bodies muffled in red and lavender triangular robes; postcards and photos; candles and vases filled with wild flowers picked from the fields. As soon as they are installed, these sparkling shards begin to interfuse their life-giving currents into the mouldering energy of the chapel, invigorating and purifying it.

We have found a large indigo blue vase in the house, shaped like a chalice; it is perfect for suggesting both the alembic, or distilling vessel, of the alchemists, and also the Holy Grail. Institutional Christianity has tried to suppress the Holy Grail and its legends, but in at least some of these legends, the Grail is considered to be the cup from which Jesus drank at the Last supper on the night of his arrest—and which Mary Magdalene is alleged to have brought with her to France. The old Provençal legends of the Sangraal describe the plight of a lonely, wounded Fisher King and the kingdom that has become a wasteland because the Grail has been lost. According to Margaret Starbird, it is the loss of the feminine counterpart of God which causes the King's mysterious wound that never heals. It derives from a sickness of the soul. "The Grail is not an artifact," she writes, "it is the lost and repudiated Bride of God . . . the Lost Bride of Jesus."

Our ritual, Lorna explains, is much more than a vague desire to commune with the mysterious figure of the Black Madonna; we are creating a new template, healing this legacy of persecution. We are consciously setting out to transform the cultural ruling principle of a male, celibate priesthood that rejects erotic intimacy as the symbol of divine love.

Now we are plunged into the real drama of our journey: a reweaving of the myths and images of masculinity and femininity that are our heritage. We are here to participate in the evolutionary healing of the patriarchy by restoring the "Lost Bride" and reclaiming her as a necessary component of any future order. It is clear to everyone here that recovery of this balance of power between masculine and feminine—the Sacred Marriage—is essential to the success of the "partnership paradigm."

After supper, we take up our places in the semicircular arrangement of chairs that surrounds our working altar, which consists of eight slender candles. In the absence of a fire, each of us has a candle

THIRTEEN

to light and work with. Because of the fragile state of the building, we are not allowed to drum. Only vibrational sounds so incredibly small they will not disturb anything can be used. We shake tiny bells and wave windchimes, as gently as trees dropping their leaves.

Lorna's topaz-colored djellaba envelops her like a mantle of congealed light. Beginning with an invocation to the four points of the compass, she breathes out smoke from her Peruvian shaman's pipe in resounding whiffs while reciting prayers. Next comes a cleansing of auras with burning sage. After we open our hearts with prayer and blessing, Lorna introduces the element of alchemical gold into our ceremony, presenting each of us with a swathe of yellow ribbon, to be placed around each individual candlestick when it is our time to work with the flame. Yellow—the *citrino*—is the final and most exalted stage of the alchemical process, signifying illumination and spiritual transformation.

At some point during these procedures, a heavy, rasping breathing invades the room. I become aware of a strange, penetrating, but unseen snoring presence. Everyone in the group is wide awake and sitting in attentive silence. I see no sign of perturbation or fear on their faces. The heavy breathing continues, like some unfathomable shadow play or supernatural burlesque, at the edge of our consciousness, without interruption, for twenty minutes.

Later I confirm that everyone else heard it and was held in suspension by this macabre manifestation, but no one could identify its source or understand what it was. Perhaps we had called forth some sleeping guardian spirit of the place with our windchimes, or smoked out a remnant genie with the jungle tobacco. Whatever that jarring and intrusive sound was, the dreaming Lord of the Flies who made it went on just long enough to raise the hair on everybody's neck—until it either ran out of oxygen or crawled back into hiding.

Fourteen

WE are roving up and down the town of Limoux in the Aude district, looking for a "miraculous Virgin" we have heard is here somewhere. The icon is not on our itinerary, but we want to find her anyway. Though we were only supposed to pass through Limoux on our way to Rocamadour, we are like hunters on the prowl, invigorated by the chase and determined, if we can, to find our prey.

It is Sunday, and also a public holiday. The first two churches we try to investigate are closed. But nobody in the group wants to give up yet. After a mediocre lunch at an outdoor café in the main square, we lay siege to one more campanile, whose turrets are visible high above the rooftops—and find that it is open.

My first glimpse of Notre-Dame de Marceille is on the wall of the religious souvenir shop just outside the church. Her picture is on a framed poster. The Madonna is smiling like a benevolent middle-aged aunt, and seems more like a suburban housewife than a Roman empress. Surprisingly different from all the others we have seen, her childlike face has no edges or angles, and no internality. She is painted a doughy gray and looks like a folk-art doll, with naïve black-button eyes that bounce straight into mine. Her head is framed by a long trail of white lace. The infant she is holding has the face of an adult and has been painted white. I can't help but wonder if the Madonna's face is gray because, at some point, it was "whitened" to rectify the unwanted darkness.

So here you are! I find myself pronouncing to the poster. We've been looking all over for you! Before entering the church, I buy postcards of her image in the souvenir shop. Once inside the church, however, looking cautiously around, all I can see are jumbo-sized statues of Jesus and Mary. The icon on the postcard is not visible anywhere.

Retracing my path back to the little shop, I gingerly ask one of the nuns in French whether the *"Vierge noire"* on the poster is to be found inside the church. Startled by my question, the nun offers to take me to the Madonna herself.

Together we reenter the church and she leads me to a recess in the wall that is hidden by heavy grillwork. So different from what I expected! This Madonna is sealed off, protected no doubt for "security" reasons, behind thick glass and imprisoning brass bars. Had she been alive, she could not have moved.

Tuning in, perhaps, to my dismay at this "caged" display, the nun explains that the Madonna is brought out on special occasions. A proprietary smile lights up her gray habit, which is the same color as the Madonna's face. In my brief silent exchange with the Madonna, I sense the emotional withering of a soul in limbo, the neglected imprisoned feminine, hidden away from the world. The nun intends to reassure me, but her words have the opposite effect, and I find myself cringing psychically against a terrible truth: the suffering of being hidden away, and the continuous violations committed against the feminine principle throughout history. Ian Begg describes this in his book very well when he says: "My impression of the reaction of the clergy to the subject of Black Virgins has been one of helpful courtesy tinged with genuine disinterest and ignorance of the subject. As a result, many of the cults are dying."

The nun smiles, defensively. She doesn't quite understand what is happening. The Madonna's face now seems oddly incomplete, unformed, washed out. I feel compelled to turn around and run, all the way out of the church.

The medieval town of Rocamadour sits at the top of a long mountain summit that has stood steadfastly through time as if all of it were set in amber. Strolling through the narrow cobblestone streets, amid the ancient buildings, one feels the signature of another world: even the stones seem to be holy.

After breakfast, we climb the 216 steps up to the chapel of Notre-Dame de Rocamadour to find the Black Madonna in whose honor the French composer Francis Poulenc composed a litany and converted to Christianity, after visiting here in 1936.

At home in her own lair, this Madonna is definitely the most archaic, sibylline, and primitive icon we have yet encountered. Not wrapped in an opulent robe like the others, her rigid walnut-brown body is stripped absolutely bare, except for the intaglio gold collar engraved on her neck. She is not a bit sensual; rather, in her maturity, the Virgin has become the Crone. Crevasses line her solemn face where layers of black paint have fermented and cracked. Her thin, bony arms rest on the rudimentary throne on which she sits, holding the Infant Deity—who looks positively middle-aged—on her knee. The lidless eyes are closed, seemingly impervious to the phenomenal world. To me she is wintry-beautiful, astringent, and a little daunting in her state of self-possession.

I find it easy to understand the explosive effect she had on Poulenc. "Alone before the pure Virgin," he wrote, "I suddenly received the indisputable sign, like a sword thrust of grace straight into the heart." A spontaneous ignition of some kind, happening right in this spot, changed him forever. Will it also happen to me? Like Poulenc, I find her presence absolutely compelling. I want to drop handfuls of lilies, sliding them one by one across her feet, like bits of prayers.

I think about the legends associated with the Black Madonna of Rocamadour—feats of miraculous rescue of sailors drowning at sea on squally nights. Models of clipper ships are rigged from the ceiling, votive offerings presented in the past by those who were grateful for the Madonna's protection. In the souvenir store below is a book, written by a monk of Rocamadour in 1192, which describes 126 miracles that occurred through her intercession. It says that the ancient chapel bell would sometimes ring miraculously, of its own accord, to calm storms when mariners in danger invoked her aid.

Now, at the very end of our journey, it seems absurd, outrageous even, that I am not looking forward to visiting Chartres. Avowedly the greatest religious monument in France, this is the Gothic cathedral in its purest, most beautiful form. But after the rareness of Rocamadour, my fear is of an unfathomable vastness overflowing with tourists; my solitary and romantic spirit will be denied the intimate communion I have met with in other places. My fellow pilgrims think I've got an attitude. None of them cares how big the crowd is.

A harsh rain dogs us from the rich valley plains of Rodamadour all the way to Chartres. Everybody else in our group wants to visit Lascaux II, a partial reconstruction of the original caves at Lascaux, which are no longer accessible to the general public. I am dead set against the plan, thinking that a fake cave would surely amount to nothing, but all the evidence is that I am outnumbered.

My worst fears are realized when we are herded briskly past bulbous hunks of synthetic rock, pausing only long enough to observe the imitation paintings while being lectured to by a guide about the technical perfection of this inanimate, sham environment, which, it seems, took eleven years to build. No dead moths or bat guano or prehistoric ooze in the interior gloom reminds us that we are supposed to be within the bowels of the earth. This environment is odor-free, completely divorced from its original counterpart. I can't help but resent the appliquéd labels, printed with dry explanations, and the hapless tourists shuffling past them in controlled groups all the way to the exit. Any sense of real spiritual magic, that once played such a significant role in the human sphere, is completely debased and falsified by this packaged experience, which is over in fifteen minutes. As we trek back to the van, I think about my friend, the potter M. C. Richards, who once described a similar episode, when, on approaching a buffet table at a conference she was attending, she discovered that the flowers she had been so admiring in the centerpiece weren't real, but only plastic. They're not flowers, she howled in anguished denunciation, her little bubble of ecstasy blown—only to find that nobody else seemed to mind at all. In our group, everybody else seems to have been enthralled with the fifteen-minute exercise.

In ancient times, Chartres was a sacred center of the Druidic world. Reflecting great honor on the town, the cathedral rises up like a phantasm out of a seemingly empty field, as you approach it from the road. Nothing on the outside, however, prepares you for the radiant blast of cobalt blue that rains down like a waterfall from gigantic stained glass windows as you enter. The luminosity is so overpowering it nearly knocks you down. And it never changes, whether the light outside is bright or gray.

We find Notre-Dame du Pilier, Our Lady of the Pillar, in a small chapel to the left of the labyrinth, placed high up on a plinth. She is bathed in vaporous pink light that seeps down from a canopy of lanterns overhead, formed by the junction of two elegant curves studded with big heart milagros made of beaten gold. Although actually seated with the Divine Child on her lap, the Black Madonna appears to be standing on the pillar, because of the huge pyramid of embroidered gold brocade that covers both their bodies in a flamboyant way. She is surrounded everywhere by a profusion of candles and flowers, creating a kind of small city on the floor around the column.

I had not foreseen that this Madonna, this flash point of spectacular divine beauty, would become the apotheosis of my journey. Tilting myself slightly forward like a magnifying glass aimed at the sun, I feel such an infusion of awe that, for a moment, there is nothing left in the universe but her and me. And in that moment, I become her secret agent.

"When you become her secret agent," Andrew Harvey writes in *The Return of the Mother*, "then everything will dance around you—you have become a lens through which her nuclear force radiates." I have come on this journey, I realize, as a way of articulating myself as a spiritual being, so that I can live spiritual consciousness and not just speculate or theorize about it. I want to experience full immersion in the phenomenon of mysticism, nothing less.

"The great secret of mystic life," says Harvey, "is trust absolute. If you trust absolutely, you will always be receptive enough to the signals that life and God and yourself will be giving you. You will always be given the clue, the information, and the inspiration to carry you through."

Radical trust is perhaps the central defining feature of the feminine consciousness. As her secret agent, my emotional bond and rapport with the Black Madonna require this level of trust, which may just be the biggest, and most demanding, action of my life. Can I let myself really do that? Trust absolutely in the rightness of whatever happens next?

As the afternoon sun blazes over Chartres cathedral, my head begins to cloud with fear and doubt. I am afraid of making mistakes. Of being disappointed again. I realize I have no idea what I am coming back to.

Returning for a last farewell to Our Lady of the Pillar, I open myself to the spiritual presence of the Madonna. Then, it's as if I hear an inner voice telling me something:

"The task is not to permit the effort to vex you. No matter how often you are disappointed, you must try to start again. Don't be sidetracked or put off by opposition. Take a stand and stick to your guns. Then let fate take its course. Allow your life to go into the hands of the universe completely."

Fifteen

ON my first day back in Tai Chi class, Tom seems glad to see me, smiling and asking me how the trip was. He looks quite pleased with the small tins of duck and goose liver paté I press into his hand.

Great, I tell him, it was really great. And there the conversation ends. Whatever dialogue I may have aspired to is over, since my unwilling mentor fails to join it. That he might want to hear my story, or ask a question, does not occur to him.

In the middle of the night, I am jolted awake by some portentous fury, flinging itself in rebellion against the spirit of spoiled patriarchal gods who refuse to acknowledge women's presence, and prefer a world where women are not. Buzzing in my memory is the oppressive constriction of the Black Madonna of Limoux, and the wild feeling that descended on me when I saw her beauty imprisoned behind bars. The revelation overtakes me that my situation mirrors hers. Suddenly a whole cultural history plays out before my inner eye, subsumed in the archetypal image of the shackled woman in the Tarot. From nowhere comes an unspoken voice, uttering these perfectly still little words: "I need to be seen, I need to be heard." With her smiling gray face adhering to my psyche like a dead barnacle, I realize it is the Black Madonna of Limoux who is speaking. Then I realize that she is also me.

There is no resisting the element of provocation set in motion by that implacable voice, demanding to be honored and given its rightful place. Some other, more ancient scenario was compelling me to ride into battle, wearing a stunning cloak of vulture feathers, and engage in a confrontational clash with the patriarchal Warrior God. This archetypal energy emanated from a much deeper stratum of the psyche than a mere grinding of my gears with Tom. Something about it embodied the dynamic and fierce heart of the dark feminine, trying to emerge as an aspect of our whole culture's unfolding reality.

"This is the great challenge of our time," Richard Tarnas writes in his influential book *The Passion of the Western Mind*, "the evolutionary imperative for the masculine to see through and overcome its hubris and one-sidedness... to choose to enter into a fundamentally new relationship of mutuality with the feminine in all its forms. The feminine then becomes not that which must be controlled, denied, and exploited, but rather fully acknowledged, respected, and responded to for itself."

As her secret agent, as an intermediary between the Black Madonna and others, encouraging that shift in attitude had become part of my cultural work: transforming the stigma of patriarchal indifference into something less traumatic—into reverence, empathy, generosity of spirit. But even with my battle energy up, I knew it couldn't be done by direct frontal assaults. The stifling situation with Tom was leading me to redefine my priorities and values on many levels.

My usual way of moving through the obstructions and disillusionments that take hold of me has been to consult the *I Ching*. Absorbing its wisdom helps me to overcome my limitations and presumptions, and to prevent mistakes. In general, the counsel is not to lash out or go to extremes, and not to strive compulsively to make things happen. Over and over again, the *I Ching* instructs me to remain tolerant and alert, and to be resolute against my fears. It grooms me for the long wait. Learning to wait has been my most profound spiritual task. It seems incredible to me the length of time I've had to wait, but the more I have used the *I Ching*, the more my belief in it has grown. It's like having my own private guide and companion, a specialized conduit for receiving spiritual energies.

Today's reading, however, arrives like a rock thrown through a plate glass window. No further progress seems possible, it says, and the finest clothes turn to rags. Expect oppression at the hands of the man with the purple knee-bands. The *I Ching* informs me that the bad times are not over. A long-established process could be eclipsed. With what seems like crushing accuracy, my psychic telescope states that I have become aware of the need of a change for the better and wish to move in that direction. But, it warns, my friends may not follow and my path could be a solitary one. The advice it delivers is to make a confident and powerful retreat.

But where do the surrendered go, and what do they do? In his wonderful study of the Tristan and Iseult myth, *We*, Robert Johnson addresses the importance of knowing when to surrender and retreat, and of doing it at the right time and in the right way: seeing the moment clearly and entering into it with the whole being. "If you are willing to pull back the projections," he writes, "although there is suffering involved, the suffering produces something. Evolution and change rather than vain repetition of the dance."

Demonstrably, the dance was closing in on me. And despite my years of *I Ching* training, a part of me was still drawn to the surgical strike: in this case, returning Tom's book. The book represented staying on course, sticking with it. No one could fault me for wanting to throw the umbrella down in the mud, fire a gunshot, and get the hell out from under. It would have the force of a moral imperative. All my sincere efforts had failed—and so, if you can't play the game to win, it is better to withdraw your energies.

To give the book back, I knew, was no peripheral detail. It stood, I intuited, for an unspoken exchange of vows. And in a manner of speaking, returning it was the stick of dynamite that could vaporize everything for which I had striven.

The truth is, I couldn't just give it all up; everything was now hooked together as if woven into a web. I had to stay in the situation long enough so that I could bring something back, a treasure that was still hidden. The story, as I had come to perceive it, was about not giving up, not yielding to setbacks or disappointment. By now it had become like a sacred scroll, endowed with its own intensity. There was a certain ritual enjoyment in the act of living out a story, and submitting it to a long process of ripening as a work of art. What I was doing seemed to me to have a divine imprint, and for this reason, returning the book was a river I couldn't step into. It almost didn't matter what Tom was doing. Even if I found myself in circumstances which were unsuccessful, profitless, or abortive, the challenge was to remain steadfast, and to trust whatever happened, to submit to everything. To leave the path was not an option—it would be worse than defeat.

"Am I prepared for what a call might bring?" David Spangler writes in *The Call*. "Because if I summon a summoning, if I invoke a call through my desire, the very worst thing I can do is then say no to it."

Without succumbing to any hard line of attack or indulging in any sweeping gestures, I would have to find some other way of bringing these two great waves of energy turning under on themselves into balance inside myself: the desire to leave the situation and the need to stay with it. Holding these contradictions was clearly part of the path.

For spiritual paths, according to Spangler, you train. "You go to the edge of what you think you can do. Then you push that edge a bit, get comfortable, then push it some more. Pretty soon you discover that the edge just keeps moving back. The flip side of every summons is transformation of the summonee."

The *I Ching* has warned me not to challenge the snake in its den, or enter its territory. My retreat will be an inner one: the will reaches a decision not to submit to being held. I go to the altar, knowing what I am going to do.

Taking the yellow ribbon from the altar drawer, I cut off a segment, which I then shear into several strands, placing the scraps, like symbolic shrapnel, inside my talismanic box, next to the vine leaf and the peach pit: a symbolic severing of the bond of union. The action is minimal, but it feels like blowing up a bridge. In grave times of struggle, the *I Ching* says, all misgivings must be silenced. This alone can "discipline the Devil's Country."

Sixteen

WHEN, in her wrathful form, the Dark Goddess rises up demanding battle against patriarchal blindness and indifference, then I have no choice. Part of the duty of the sacred feminine is to protect the earth against willful destruction; pledged as Her agent, I can never turn away from this responsibility. Right now, in another scene of crisis, this blind patriarchal will is playing out the drama of environmental destruction just seven miles from my front door.

Virginia Polytechnic Institute and State University, Blacksburg's educational headquarters, is poised to scythe through one of the most beautiful valleys in the state of Virginia. The plan is to begin construction on a "smart" highway—a six mile, fiber-optic bridge, to be used for testing new intelligent vehicle technologies. This enterprise is inseparably linked with another "pork-barrel" road project: to run a major interstate highway right through the town. With the intention of bringing to themselves important national acclaim and lucrative research contracts, the university is inflicting their high-tech project on a reluctant local population hardly even aware of what is going on.

The moral isn't new, or for some people, even arresting. It is assumed, in our virile culture, that to damage, scar, and pollute in the name of economic growth, technological development, and more jobs, is just "the way things are." As soon as the bulldozers and the cranes come, the natural environment will be shredded into rags. Our once secure and pastoral valley will not just be dominated by the gigantic, overhead concrete bridge of the "smart road"—soon to be the tallest bridge in Virginia—it will literally be consumed by the presence of seventy-two snow-making machines, power-driven by noisy diesel air compressors and water pumps, rising forty feet into the air and releasing four inches of snow every hour to simulate blizzards and icy road conditions. All of this flamboyant paraphernalia will be part of an experimental program of all-weather road-testing, intended to promote fiber-optic technology, a major field of research at the university.

Dedicated to high-level, cutting-edge technology, and to increasing corporate profits, the university doesn't care about "ecological virtue." It wants to make its own statement, even though this means taking over a hundred and forty acres of legally "protected" agricultural land in the valley. The University is not concerned with rolling pasture or organic totalities, with living trees or seedlings or lichens; consequently they will alter the valley beyond recognition. These acts of indifference, repeated over and over, are like a destructive poison in our civilization's emotional body.

Tonight, the local Board of Supervisors is going to vote on whether or not they will condemn this land and hand it over to the University for their Faustian pursuits. There is a public meeting in which the intellectual pros and cons of constructing the "smart road" will be discussed, giving the impression that everyone's input is being considered. Tonight, as Her secret agent and seeing the world as She sees it, I am the valley which is under siege. I am the squirrels and the worms, the trees which will die when the bulldozers come. And for what it is worth, I have a three-minute slot in which to stand up to the patriarchal will and speak Her truth. Once again I am wondering, with an adrenaline surge, how I can penetrate the stigma of this indifference. Is there any way to transform arrogant blindness into something simpler or sweeter—into reverence? Because this, I now understand, is what the feminine principle, working through me, is trying to achieve. And one of the penalties of ecological sensitivity, as Aldo Leopold pointed out years ago in *A Sand County Almanac,* is that you must be the doctor who sees the marks of death in a community that believes itself well and does not want to be told otherwise.

When my name is called, I stand before the President of the University, the Board of Supervisors, representatives of the Commonwealth Boards of Transportation and Chamber of Commerce, and the land developers, all of whom want the highway and believe in it, without the least hesitation, as their living myth. Scattered among this corporate elite are many stricken members of the community, ordinary citizens who understand their place within this beauty and its necessity within their lives. Holding placards which say "The Smart Road Is Dumb," they look haunted.

I am not optimistic—to love the land is seen as a kind of anachronistic curiosity in today's growth-oriented culture. I will be talking to people for whom the intoxicating lure of jobs and increased productivity is the formula that makes life fulfilling and worthwhile. They are prepared to do whatever it takes to win.

When it is finally my turn, I ask them not to do it, not to follow the assumption they have always followed, that money and technological advance are the only path to a successful future, the only true indicators of a community's well-being and prosperity. We are already on the brink of global ecological collapse because of our incessantly expanding needs and preoccupation with economic growth and technological progress. At least let there be a public referendum before we succumb to a bulldozing frenzy.

From the speaker's podium on the aisle I have a direct view of the seven members of the Board of Supervisors, who are seated, listening, at a long table on the stage. Six are men, one is a woman. It is already known that three of the men are supporters of the road, and three are not. The revolving wild card here, holding the swing vote in her hand like a sprig of fresh lilac, is Mary Biggs, a schoolteacher and newcomer to the Board. She is not the puffy-faced bureaucrat I was expecting, but has the serene face of the Virgin Mary from a Quattrocento painting. For a moment I see her as an inexperienced miracle worker who just might walk on water and save the valley.

The supervisors look directly at me with wary curiosity. All, that is, except for Mary Biggs, whose sober brown eyes seem to sanction what I am saying in their depths, and to encourage me. I find myself absolutely gripped and fascinated by the implications of her fate and burden as the one person who can make a difference. Will her conscience stipulate that she fiercely defend and protect the beauty of her countryside? Or will she be caught in the snare of "smart road" techno-psychology and vote to squander it?

That night, Mary Biggs didn't walk on water. The valley was handed over to its new managers—individuals who will, in an extraordinary display of opportunistic greed, subject their trophy to ordeals of degradation, noise, and pollution, in a bargain that, I realize now, had been struck already well in advance of the public hearing by those who command the field. In retrospect, it seems as if Mary Biggs's vote was only fulfilling the laws of its being, not coinciding with a real choice so much as the channeling of her feminine effectiveness into the momentum of a foregone conclusion.

A few days after the fateful countdown, I find myself wondering whether Mary Biggs is feeling any sorrow or remorse at the thought of what she has done. I decide to write her a letter. Having just read an article in *Resurgence*, an environmental magazine published in England, which describes the grisly wheeling-and-dealing that went on behind the scenes in a somewhat similar circumstance of highway building in Ireland, I want to let Mary Biggs know that I am not "unaware" of the hypocrisy and fraudulence I now see also infused the proceedings around the "smart road." It is obviously part of the dilemma those who wish to preserve what is left of the environment must now confront: the fact that mega-road deals such as this one are decided well in advance at the highest levels of state government, and no amount of citizen input would ever have a chance of derailing it. Public hearings of the sort I attended are just a smoke screen to give local residents the false impression of having a say. The real truth is that

SIXTEEN

none of us, Mary Biggs included, were ever really in the loop. In part, I want to convey to Mary Biggs my compassion for her plight.

Tacked up on the wall above my desk as I write to Mary Biggs is the photograph of Sara, patron saint of the Gypsies, that I took in the church that day in Les Saintes-Maries-de-la-Mer. It is there as a powerful transmitter of the "feminine ray" coming back into manifestation and challenging male-dominated philosophies. Sara's warm piercing eyes look at me with an effort of deep attention. In a shock of recognition, I recognize their resemblance to Mary Biggs's eyes, which had looked at me that night in the same way. In fact, the physiological likeness between the two faces is hard to avoid. The discovery feels profound, even a little uncanny. It prompts me to include a copy of the photograph with my letter. And then, without any sure sense of where all this might be headed, I invite Mary Biggs to lunch.

Many months pass, without any response from Mary Biggs. Then one afternoon as I am sitting at my desk revising my account of this story, and still trying to penetrate the meaning of events that surrounded Mary Biggs's action, the telephone rings. At the other end of the receiver, a voice says, "This is Mary Biggs."

What can we truly know about the mystery of how the universe works? Was the precise timing of this call just an "accidental" occurrence? When she received my letter eight months ago, rather than answering it, Mary Biggs had put my name on a list of people to notify about some new proposals being put forward with regard to rezoning laws in the County. These proposals were due to be aired publicly before the Board of Supervisors in a few days, and Mary Biggs was calling to invite me to the meeting.

I seize the chance to ask about my letter, and how it felt to be the lone female protagonist in a land drama that was going to put our beautiful green expanse to such shameful uses.

There was, in Mary Biggs's response to my question, no unspoken discomfort, no hidden pocket of caution or subterfuge. Nor was there any sign of real anguish for the world's warring paradigms concerning the environment either. Without fuss, Mary Biggs acknowledged that she had enjoyed my letter and had even saved the photograph. As for being the decisive player in the flawed saga of the "smart road," or undergoing any personal crisis over it herself, after our conversation I could see that Mary Biggs never saw her role in that light.

As far as I could tell, all the symbolic implications and passionate utopian hopes I had attributed to her task were in actuality entirely absent from Mary Biggs's own experience of the event. Overwhelmed by the huge amounts of data that had come her way only late in the day, she had struggled to acquire a good working grasp of the pros and cons of the situation, much the way an accountant works to figure taxes, applying the same kinds of terms and methods. And in that countinghouse, the pros carried the day. Big business won control of the valley.

Still, the synchronous phone call was persuasively eloquent for me—a sign that uncanny threads of fate weave together inner and outer experience in a way that no rational explanation can ever fully penetrate.

Seventeen

I STARTED OUT in Virginia with the agenda of consciously bringing more magic into my life, but as I look back and reexamine my own history over the years, I can see that magic, as a special gift in the form of miraculous synchronicity, has actually been there all along.

The synchronous phone call from Mary Biggs has shaken up memories of other meaningful coincidences that shifted and shaped my course, often with no more than the slightest flicker of movement. In the past, I considered them only as isolated events, appearing suddenly from nowhere, totally by chance. More recently, I have come to accept synchronicity as an indwelling and organic principle, orchestrating, from infinitely subtle levels, each life-changing twist and turn of fate.

"It is an audacious notion to put forth in this age of science and willful determination that one's existence is somehow inspired, guided, and even managed by unseen forces outside our control," Robert Johnson has written in his memoir, *Balancing Heaven and Earth*. I don't claim to understand what these unseen forces are. They baffle the rational mind. But I am more and more convinced that what Johnson says is true. Life may appear to be random on the surface, but at a deeper level, it is completely organized. Magic, arriving often in the form of synchronicity, is the part we do not control or could not have predicted.

I was just out of school, in my early twenties, having graduated with a Bachelor of Arts degree from Hunter College in New York, and had applied for a Fulbright scholarship to go to Belgium. On one level I was seeking adventure and a way to experience the culture of Europe. I was also convinced I had the perfect project for winning a grant, which was to write a book about the Belgian surrealist painter René Magritte, who was little known at that time. This undertaking would require traveling to Brussels, where Magritte lived, to do the research.

Excitement soon turned to despondency, however, when I failed to get the grant. But by that time, through the intercession of a friend, I was in correspondence with Magritte, who had written a letter to me about his passion for American detective novels. I remember that he asked me to describe, as best I could, the precise contents of an American hamburger, which the characters in these novels were always eating. As our correspondence flourished, Magritte seemed genuinely enthusiastic to have a young amanuensis from America show up on his doorstep. But I had no money to get there.

And then, out of the blue came a phone call, with its brief but unexpected bestowal. At the other end of the line, someone informed me that a Persian rug I had put into storage in the warehouse of a department store, because it didn't fit into the apartment where I was living, had been badly damaged by a fire. The voice announced that a check would arrive in the mail very shortly from the insurance company to cover the loss.

With the money from my "magic carpet," I booked myself a passage to Antwerp on a Norwegian freighter, and arrived in Belgium a few months later, wearing a knitted crimson beret. The Magrittes, René and Georgette and their Pomeranian dog Loulou, were all on the quai waiting for me. Magritte couldn't drive and didn't own a car, so we took the train back to Brussels. And thus began my nine-month odyssey as *"la jeune fille américaine,"* the young American woman who was living in Magritte's attic while writing a book about him. I was twenty-five years old when I was propelled into writing this biography, without ever having done anything like it before. The anxiety was intense, but so was the excitement.

Most mornings Magritte painted in the large dressing room just outside his bedroom. The floor was fully carpeted, yet there were never any paint stains on it. With a degree of wit and humor, Magritte loved to feign boredom in the extreme while he was painting. "*Que je m'ennuie*," he would sigh into the smoke of his cigarette, as though longing to discover the possibility of a different destiny. One day, I found him painting a huge green apple, with the inscription "This is not an apple" underneath it. When I saw it, immediately I smiled.

"But it's not funny," he said. "It's accurate."

Early on during my stay, there was an exhibition of Magritte's paintings in the town of Charleroi, where he was born. Quantities of champagne, *croque monsieurs*, and smoked eels were served at the opening. Magritte was as bored by openings as he was by painting. Distraction could be supplied by the artful practical joke, which he did not neglect to cultivate. On this occasion, bandits in cahoots, we amused ourselves together by trying to dupe a rather tedious pushy woman into believing that I was the visiting chief of a tribe of North American Indians. Failing to notice our suppressed giggles, she took the bait.

Despite these occasional subversions, the days were usually orderly and clear, with Magritte painting in the mornings, while I studied and wrote. Then, after a big lunch and a nap, we would travel downtown from the suburbs by tram, and Magritte would go to play chess at the Café Greenwich. One day I invited him to join me and a friend at the Café des Marionettes in the Grand Place instead, thinking he might enjoy a change of scene.

"Oh no," he assured me. "I prefer chess. And you? I suppose you prefer marionettes!"

Occasionally he would sacrifice his chess game for an afternoon matinée with Georgette. One rainy day the three of us went to see a Brigitte Bardot movie, in which she plays a dropout hippie who murders her musician husband after he tells her that he never loved her. I expect I was the only one taken in by the pathos of the story. Magritte hated the film, and walked out in the middle to head for the Greenwich. "*Une histoire de conçierge,*" he said later, in his most debunking tone and flashing an anarchic grin. A story for janitors, absolutely without merit.

The high point of each week was the Saturday night gathering of friends, at the center of which was Magritte's great *amigo*, the writer Jean Scutenaire, a cordial, witty, intelligent man with no hair, who reminded me of a tallish Jean Genet. Scut always had a cigarette dangling from his mouth, Bogart-style, and although he never smoked, it would get shorter and shorter as he periodically cut off the soggy butt end. Then, throwing it away, he would replace the discarded cigarette with another.

At our Saturday night gatherings, Magritte's latest painting would be inspected and admired, and suggestions for a title solicited. Scut always came up with the best titles, but there was one occasion when mine was the winner, and I received a small gouache of the painting as a reward. The image was that of a lone tree situated on a background of leaves. My title was "*L'Arc de Triomphe.*"

At one point, in an exceedingly interesting digression, Magritte became excited about making home movies. He went out and purchased a lot of expensive equipment and spent much of the week composing a "script," based on the images in his paintings.

When Saturday night arrived, we all took part in the drama. My role was to sit in a chair, wearing a red carnival mask over my eyes, giving birth to a tuba, which emerged slowly from under my skirt. Playing the part of a hunchback thief, Scut ran around the house stealing Magritte's paintings, hilariously outfitted in a striped Mexican dress that belonged to me, with a pillow stuffed in his back for a hump, and my red knitted beret on top of his bald head. Years later this movie was shown as a short accompanying the favorite film of the surrealists about Dracula, *Nosferatu*, in conjunction with a big exhibition on Dada and Surrealism on view at the

SEVENTEEN

Hayward Gallery in 1978.

Without Scut's help, I might never have completed my task. Although there was a huge gap in our ages, and despite the fact that he was married as well, Scut became infatuated with me from the moment we met. Every week I would visit him in his den, where he allowed me to pore over his Magritte archive and inducted me into the fantastic world of surrealism. Secretly we would meet during the day in his favorite haunts; mostly deserted cafés where, for a few stolen hours in the afternoon, we would drink wine and concentrate on kissing. I must confess that this affectionate attention was like a warming Gulf Stream that helped me to survive the otherwise dark, wet, and melancholic Belgian winter. Often I would receive long love poems in French, which took me hours of hard labor to decipher. We developed, during that year, a remarkable friendship, and on the day that I left Brussels for good, Scut wept.

Thinking about all of this now, it seems amazing that the entire string of events came about as the result of a single, random phone call. Today, being more attuned to the spiritual aspects of synchronicity, I recognize something more like the "butterfly effect" from chaos theory, which describes the dramatic influence that small changes can have on large systems through underlying webs of relationship: a butterfly flapping its wings in Beijing may cause a cyclone in Brazil. In my case, that one phone call became a fractal thread unwinding its effects throughout my whole life across a network of interconnected events. It was even the catalyst that got me to Virginia, almost thirty years later.

For instance, during the year I lived with Magritte in Brussels, I stumbled upon several of his discarded works in the attic, which he then gave me as a gift. One of them was a rogue drawing in pencil, of a man who was being pursued from behind by a bunch of flying knives and forks. When I returned to New York and showed the drawing to Jasper Johns, I could see that he fell in love with it and wanted very much to have it. So I proposed to trade it for something by him. He agreed and asked me what I wanted.

About six months later, I received what I had asked for: a small encaustic Flag painting. It had been made specially for me, painted on top of a child's flag bought in Woolworth's, and it had a photostrip of my face collaged onto the surface. I was seized up with excitement and disbelief, now the owner of one of the most spectacular and sought-after icons in modern Western civilization.

I owned the painting for more than twenty years before deciding to sell it. I decided to sell it because I wanted to leave London for good and return to America, and I didn't have the money to make a big move.

Originally I had hoped to live in Santa Barbara. Since I'd been teaching on and off at the university there, the possibility of a long-term appointment developed under the genial influence of a certain thoughtful dean. But he couldn't make good on the plan, since it was sabotaged by a clutch of hostile professors in the art department, who felt threatened by my provocative ideas. Doggedly they chewed away at the situation until it finally caved in. When my dream collapsed, I was devastated. I had no prospects for the future and no idea of where I should go instead. A month later there was another out-of-the-blue phone call. It was an invitation to teach for a year at Virginia Tech in Blacksburg, as the C. C. Garvin Endowed Professor at the College of Arts and Sciences. After I got to Blacksburg, I decided to stay, and some months later, with the money I had received from the sale of the painting, I bought my house. All of this happened, I now see, through the amazing "butterfly effect" of that quite unrelated, but nevertheless pivotal phone call advising me, nearly forty years ago now, that my Persian rug had burned up in storage.

We tend to think of life as being unpredictable and random, rather like the weather, a chain of unconnected experiences flowing like an arrow through time. A closer look has convinced me that life is more like an ecosystem than a linear equation: all the parts are interconnected. This feeling for the relationship *between* things—seeing the world as a cat's cradle of interconnections rather than as a set of isolated fragments—is something I learned from being a collage artist: everything is related to everything else. Nothing is isolated. Nothing exists separately from all the rest. And synchronicities are the nodal points, magic moments where seemingly unrelated events are woven together to form a single, undivided world fabric.

Eighteen

THE thing that I remember most of all about the years after I returned to New York from Brussels was the sickening struggle and humiliation I felt at not being able to find a publisher for the Magritte manuscript. Although I'd written occasional art reviews for *Art News*, in those days if you were a young woman, things were grim. Publishing was a man's world, and I was still an unpublished writer, caught up in momentum of being a celebrated example of nothing. It felt like the doors of the world were all set against me. Things were made even more complicated by the fact that I was also trying to make my way as a collage artist and become established in the art world. In those days one could be one or the other, artist or writer, but professionalism demanded a sharp choice. Trying to combine both practices and keep the energy moving in two directions only muddied the waters, and was a tricky business.

I am astonished now to think how persistently I was obsessed with my goal, as much from rectitude as from anything else. Whatever the odds stacked against me, I felt a deep obligation to all the people who had helped me, especially Magritte, and I wanted to bring the project to a successful conclusion. Like a belligerent monkey in slippery circumstances, I scrambled around every luckless possibility for publication that I could find, to no avail. When all of my most determined efforts finally went down the tubes, I grew quite desperate at not being able to "make" it happen.

The final nail in the coffin came when, in 1964, the Museum of Modern Art announced a major retrospective of Magritte's work, and it was agreed that he would journey to the U.S. for the first time to attend the opening. In my mind, I imagined that since I had already put in several years of work on the subject, refracted through my special access to a very private archive, the catalogue essay would be mine to write. It wouldn't be as effective as a book, but at least my efforts would be vindicated.

The truth is that I never even had a chance. The Museum chose their long-time employee, James Thrall Soby, who had already authored distinguished books on two other surrealist artists—Giorgio de Chirico and Yves Tanguy—to write the text. Soby was a seasoned and highly respected "good old boy." There was no way I could have competed with such a robustly established figure.

One day I had a telephone call from Soby, asking if we could meet. It turned out he didn't know Magritte, and even feigned a certain diffidence about the task he now found in front of him. We chatted quite amiably for a while, and then, removing the veneers of the moment, Soby disclosed the real purpose of his visit. He wanted to borrow my text. "Of course if I end up using any of it, I'll make sure you have full credit in a footnote," he assured me.

It was one of those existential situations, as if one were suddenly face-to-face with a boa constrictor or a lion. The prospect of all my passion and dedication being reduced to a polite footnote in someone else's text extended itself like a cold weather front across my heart. I didn't exactly want to be unhelpful to Soby, since he seemed like a nice enough person and since it wasn't, after all, his fault that my efforts hadn't succeeded. But—I was perfectly candid—there was no way I could agree to this form of subjugation. Somehow I found the presence of mind to speak the dramatically appropriate utterance: no thanks.

To his everlasting credit, Soby was sympathetic. And then, in an unguarded moment, he gave away the secret of his own ordeal. The first manuscript he'd ever written, when he was still young—a commissioned work about Impressionism—had also never been published. To that day, he told me, it was still locked away in a suitcase.

EIGHTEEN

Odd as it may seem, hearing his story "cured" me of my obsessive need to publish. Throwing in the towel, yielding with good grace to defeat, simply turning my back on the whole unbearable affair, had simply never occurred to me.

Today I understand that when something in your life isn't working, it may be a sign that the universe has something else in mind. Other things were going badly, too. The apartment building where I lived got sold, and I was evicted. The free-lance editorial work which was my main source of income petered out. What I thought was a glowing love affair abruptly ended. In the midst of all my exasperation and trauma, I received some kind of inner instruction in the form of a message: if you can just get to London, everything will be all right. It was a simple inspiration, spoken by a voiceless voice that seemed to come from inside my head.

I wanted to go. London during the late 1960s was a fashionable and "swinging" cultural milieu, the custodian of Pop culture. I liked the idea of living abroad, but I also wanted to be where people spoke English. New York, I felt, was sucking my life away. London promised a lively ambience, and the possibility of disposing of all my problems by simply recreating myself elsewhere.

Finally I decided to cut my losses. With some help from my best friend at the time, a fashion photographer who had moved to London with her husband the previous year so he could study psychoanalysis at the Anna Freud Clinic, I rented a "bedsitter," a single room with shared bathroom in a large, red-brick Victorian mansion, a block away from the Swiss Cottage Tube station and quite near the public library. The rent was a mere twenty-four dollars a week, which included a big English breakfast. There was a cool, grassy garden at the back bordered by flowers, where I could read and write. After eight years of hacking it in New York, the feeling of heaviness vanished rapidly. This was like being at a spa.

I had arrived in London with nothing but my clothes, a typewriter, and the names of three art critics to call, supplied by Thomas B. Hess, at that time the editor of *Art News*, one of the few magazines which had published my work. Everything else had been put into storage or stashed with friends, including the luckless manuscript, which, taking my cue from Soby's story, had landed in someone's musty basement.

One of the names on my exemplary little list was that of John Russell, who was then the art critic for the London *Sunday Times*. John was all elegance and grace, watered silk ties and English wit. He was also married, albeit not happily. His worldliness, intelligence, and sophistication were a great lure, as were the bouquets of tall yellow roses, which began to arrive regularly at the red-brick mansion, discreetly set out for my return on the hall table by my landlady, together with the mail. It wasn't long before the key was turned in the lock and my life became an entranced circle, with John at its center.

One day I told John the long sad saga of my benighted manuscript, and how, despite all my pushing, demanding, compelling, and leaving no stone unturned, nothing had worked out. His response was to introduce me to his publisher. As it turned out, they were actually on the prowl for someone who could write a book about Magritte. Thus, eight years later, my publisher just appeared, whether by good luck or magic or the leftover force of my original desire, flowing now through a different channel, in England.

John and I had a rich and stimulating art-world life together in London for six years, until it all spilled on the ground one day when he announced that he was in love with someone else and went off to live with her in New York, where he eventually got married and became a staff writer for the *New York Times*. For months I wailed and wept and dragged myself through what must surely have been the bitterest, most painful year of my life. But the pity I saw in other people's eyes began to alarm me. It was like having a glimpse of oneself in a storefront window and not liking what one saw. Being looked upon as a betrayed, "abandoned" woman was serving me badly and had become an impediment to my life. In that moment of depleting vision, I made a choice. I chose not to be dragged under any longer by my suffering, but to come through it, to wipe it away with the back of my hand. Once I got used to it, the choice set me free, and my agony ended. Needing a break after that unhappy hardscrabble ordeal, I began to emerge from the darkness. Suddenly I was in clear space, and I looked around me for signs of life.

Nineteen

AFTER JOHN LEFT, an entirely new period in my life was initiated, by yet another phone call that arrived out of nowhere, bearing my future aloft on its own unwinding strand of events. The call was from the American Embassy, and the voice at the other end of the line belonged to a program director for the USIS (at that time known as the United States Information Services) who was proposing to send me to Hungary to give lectures about contemporary American art. The invitation was a bit of a fluke—the person they really wanted to send was unable to go and had proposed me as a possible substitute instead. At that point I hadn't done much public lecturing, but the prospect of visiting Budapest, the city my father had been born in, seemed provocative, so I agreed to go.

In itself, the trip to Hungary would not have been a life-changing event, except that it led subsequently to a whole series of lecture tours in much more exotic places like Nepal, Bangladesh, Sri Lanka, India, Pakistan, Egypt, Jordan, and Turkey. I found myself pushed out into the world, traveling in a mode that was both glamorous and eye-opening. I was invited, in my new emissary role, to explain the mystique of modern art—and bridge the gap in understanding that exists between people outside the professional art world and those within it.

At first it was daunting, and even a little embarrassing, trying to describe to avid crowds of mostly local, indigenous artists and critics in the Third World, some of the aggressively absurd forms of art that dominated the decade of the 1970s in America: Vito Acconci putting a match to his breast and burning the hair off his chest; Chris Burden crawling half-naked across broken glass, or having himself shot in the arm by a friend with a .22-caliber rifle just so he would know what it was like to be shot; firebricks meticulously laid out in a line across the floor; monochrome canvases with no lines or images. It was hard not to be overwhelmed by the bizarreness of the situation. But I threw myself wholeheartedly into the task—which brought me in contact with many extraordinary people, quite a few of whom had studied art in the West.

Something about this experience was disconcerting, however. I began to notice that in cultures whose features were radically dissimilar to my own, artists were often willing to "destroy" their own cultural past in order to become galley slaves to a Western tradition of modernism that had been presented to them with the categorical imperative of universal aesthetic truth. I began to question why artists would want to undermine their own authority and uniqueness, in order to become derivatives of Western modernism by "faking" it. How can this be understood, I wondered, and in this unexpected blunt encounter with the "colonial" experience, I found myself becoming skeptical about the very assumptions I had set out to explain.

Once I had experienced my own culture from the outside, as it were, and then returned to it enriched by the palpable essence of others, I had to confront a simple truth: modernism, which had had such good beginnings, and which had meant so much to me, was losing its bite. The transgressive spirit of the avant-garde had been co-opted by corporate managers and was being watered to a gray wash by professional marketers of art. In the problematic cultural ambience in which I was living, modernism had suffered a certain moral lapse. Its spiritual authority and its social purpose had been lost to the tyranny of economic self-seeking.

My gallivanting odyssey in the Third World ended as abruptly as it began. The American government instituted a policy change regarding speakers, and my good friend at the Embassy in London, who had organized all my trips, got reposted to a different city. But by that time, after nearly two years of traveling, the damage had been done. Cross-cultural experiences had destabilized my belief in many commonly accepted notions associated with modernity—alienated individualism, cultural imperialism, and economic self-seeking—as being true for all time and good for all people. The impact of bringing these assumptions to light in a foreign context had opened up the possibility that some of them were limited, elitist, or just plain wrong.

As I then came to see it, modernism, and its related capitalist-imperialist world-view, were due for reappraisal. *Has Modernism Failed?*, which I began to write in 1979, reflected my struggle to answer the question of whether modernism had succeeded, or whether, in fact, it had failed. Were we leaving behind, as the modern age waned, a period of success and resonant creativity, or one of impoverishment and decline? The more I went into it, the more I realized that I was, myself, living these questions as I wrote them, undergoing my own acute crisis of credibility about the core values of Western culture—secularism, individualism, bureaucracy, and pluralism. By the time I finished writing the book, I had become a dissident voice. The modernism that had seemed so meaningful once no longer captivated me, and even seemed a little absurd.

Along with others of my generation, I was trained to view art as a specialized pursuit, devoid of practical or social goals. The concept of "art for art's sake"—art's inherent purposelessness—was not to be tinkered with, like theological law. Patriarchal philosophy declared art to be self-sufficient and "value-free." Artists cultivated the image of themselves as eccentric loners, held in suspension by art's protective bubble.

I can still remember, as though it were an ice crystal stuck inside my brain, my own induction into modern aesthetics, and how much it affected me. It took place in a seminar class taught by the painter Robert Motherwell when I was a student at Hunter College, more than forty years ago. A lively man with clever, prudent eyes and a sensual mouth, Motherwell would arrive in class every week, and I would shake with excitement at beginning my worldly life in the embrace of modern art, with one of its divine immortals as my spirit guide.

A whole semester was spent in an all-consuming study of a single essay, "The Dehumanization of Art," written by the Spanish philosopher Ortega y Gasset in 1925. This commanding text was read like scripture by the Abstract Expressionists. The title refers to the removal of all human content from art. What sticks out in my mind, beyond this shearing clean of human elements, was Ortega's description of modern art as "disinterested play"—a sort of prodigious game whose primary purpose was in mastering the game itself. He put no spin on his words. Modern art, he claimed, was "a thing of no consequence," "ill-equipped to take on the salvation of mankind." A present-day artist, Ortega said, would be thunderstruck if he were entrusted with so enormous a mission.

We still live in the fallout from this philosophy. In an exchange with a critic from the *New York Times* during his 1955 retrospective at the Guggenheim Museum, the painter Georg Baselitz was asked, more than half a century later, what role he thinks art plays in society. As if speaking from a time capsule, Baselitz replied, "The same role as a good shoe, nothing more." Perfect fuel for the engine of the NEA to reduce its funding for the arts.

It would be hard to credit a man of creative enterprise and stature with such a statement, except that it is perfectly expressive of its period. With an exactly similar breeziness, the same artist declared on another occasion: "The idea of changing or improving the world is alien to me and seems ludicrous. Society functions, and always has, without the artist. No artist has ever changed anything for better or worse." Remarks like this, tossed out casually into the cultural atmosphere, are lethally radiating in their effect. But somehow for me, these words became like a rallying cry in reverse. They made me crazy, but they also helped me to break new ground.

Even though I had, in a sense, walked right out of the official culture by saying things that many people did not want to hear, the publication of *Has Modernism Failed?* in 1984 propelled me into the public realm. It was as if a chute gate had swung open, releasing a flood of invitations to lecture and teach. My own disenchantment with the modernist myths of hard-edged individualism and "value-free" aesthetics had struck a resonant chord with artists all over the northern hemisphere, many of whom were suffering from an acute sense of isolation and from the lack of any meaningful context for their work beyond the seductive lure of the marketplace.

At that time, it was very difficult to get one's bearings outside of the mainstream and the patriarchal culture. There was a charged silence around any discussion of the artist's role in society, and no defense against brute isolation. Basically there were two options: belong to the silent universe of the unrecognized, shut up completely in one's own cocoon; or scramble up the success ladder in the art world, once described rather crisply and unforgivingly by Georgia O'Keeffe as "the pigpen."

Neither of these alternatives appealed to me. I was groping for something that might offer more dignity and truth. But to find a new direction—one that didn't revert to social alienation and embraced the idea of art serving cultural needs—required a willingness to abandon old programming. It meant coming to terms with the dense growth of beliefs that had conditioned and defined the artist's identity in modern culture as an alienated and marginal outsider. These beliefs, I now saw, had become outmoded and oppressive, and often nullifying in their effects. With its one-sided, exaggerated emphasis on individualism and freedom, modernism had managed to destroy the social self. Conditioned to live in their own world, artists frequently ended up, as Andy Warhol soberingly put it, "making things for people that they don't need."

At some point I suppose I realized that *Has Modernism Failed?* was just a curtain raiser, the prelude to another book. What I was moving towards was a new interpretation of the relationship between artist and society, based on a sense of ethical responsibility toward the social and environmental communities. What I had discovered was that I was swimming in the same sea with many others, who were also were turning their backs on the disengaged, morally neutered consciousness of modernity. The socially entrenched scenarios of innovative style, fashion, and competitive consumerism as a way of life were being challenged by other possibilities that included an altogether different topology of art as creative work in service to the whole. I didn't quite realize it yet, but I was already standing at an edgy distance from my own next big venture as a writer.

Twenty

AS I LOOK BACK on it all now, I must have been ready for a radical change, because it almost seems as if I was being launched on a preordained course. One day in a bookstore in New York's Soho, I stumbled upon a book that launched my thinking once and for all in a new direction. Written by an author I had never heard of, Marilyn Ferguson, it was called *The Aquarian Conspiracy: Personal and Social Transformation in the 1980s.* The book was an eye-opening account of well-educated professionals in many spheres who were shedding the "old position" of social alienation and self-seeking, and allowing the perils and forebodings of planetary crisis to penetrate their hearts. As a result, their lives had turned in the direction of healing and service instead of in pursuit of the standard values of corporate capitalism. In search of commitment and connection, they wanted to make a difference, and they were.

What linked the people in Ferguson's book together was their commitment to personal and social transformation—not any outer organization. But something had struck home with telling effect in Ferguson's account: conspicuously absent from these social visionaries were any examples of artists. The full force of this perception took years to digest and integrate into the narrative of my own life. But it was hardly surprising, after half a century in which the art world avoided social and moral imperatives, that the risk and excitement of social change was happening elsewhere. Art was out of the loop.

Some time after that, another book also had a profound effect on me: Thomas Berry's *Dream of the Earth*. Reading this book, I had a sudden, shocking realization of just how callous and harmful our "no limits," self-serving way of life is to the ecosphere—a recognition at the deepest levels of the severity of humanity's impact on the planet. The momentum of awakening from my own past conditioning of benign neglect was like mentally falling through a trap door. I really got it that this beautiful world is dying and that not too many people cared.

Yet I have to ask myself whether my book, *The Reenchantment of Art*, would ever have been written if the universe hadn't taken the next step. One spring day in 1988, while I was teaching in Santa Barbara, a flyer appeared in my mailbox from the Ojai Foundation. It announced some workshops to be given by Marilyn Ferguson and Riane Eisler, the author of another seminal book of the 1980s, *The Chalice and the Blade*.

I'd never heard of the Ojai Foundation, and to this day have no idea how that flyer showed up. But if I was in need of further evangelization, this was like a lighthouse beacon beaming me in. Ojai was only an hour's drive across the wide hill-country from Santa Barbara, and so, with distinctly nervous excitement, I went with a friend to attend Ferguson's workshop.

Birds were flying in and out of the ancient grove of walnut trees which flank the rough road circling up to the Foundation as we drove in. Following the signs to the parking area, we left the car and walked into the compound, which is basically no more than a loose arrangement of yurts and teepees, tucked away under the foliage. No ordinary buildings were to be seen. One yurt in particular seemed to be the gathering spot. People were sitting inside it silently, cross-legged on cushions on the floor. They were focused on Marilyn Ferguson. We melted into the silence, immediately engaged by her admirable directness and lucidity.

My attention soon became riveted on the presence of another woman, however, who was seated near Ferguson. She seemed to burn with a gemlike flame and projected a palpable spiritual poise. Dressed in a white jumpsuit, she had long, honey-colored hair pulled back in a ponytail. I found her beautiful, with a potent spiritual charge that left me quite breathless. I wondered who she was.

TWENTY

Eventually things broke up for lunch. I stood outside the yurt with my friend, wondering what to do next. The woman in the white jumpsuit came outside, too, and was engaged in thoughtful exchanges with a succession of people, who seemed to be greedy for her attention. An irresistible desire to make contact with this person took hold of me, but I was at a loss to know what I could possibly say that would cause her to notice me. I couldn't think of anything.

Finally it was my turn, and she stretched out her hand to introduce herself. Her name was Joan Halifax, and she was the director of the Ojai Foundation—the guru of the place.

I would never have recognized her name, except that on our way in, we had stopped briefly at the Foundation's little gift store, in one of the other yurts. Prominently on display was a book by Joan Halifax called *Shamanic Voices*. On the book's cover is an image of an orange snake that is coiled up underneath an orange moon, glowing in a dark purple sky. It is a reproduction of one of my collages.

Ten years before my visit to Ojai, when I was still living in London, I had received another of my out-of-the-blue phone calls. It was from a publisher in New York, who informed me that one of their authors, whose name was Joan Halifax, had seen a collage of mine reproduced in an obscure picture book. Insisting that this was the image she wanted for her cover, she told the publisher that nothing else would do. On the other end of the line, he was obviously relieved at having tracked me down. I agreed to send them a transparency, they sent me a small payment, and one day, about a year later, I received a copy of the book. But I never read it. At the time, I knew nothing about shamanism. I probably wouldn't even have remembered the author's name, except that I had just seen the book displayed in the gift store.

"You're Joan Halifax?" I cried in astonishment. "Then I think it's my work which is on the cover of your book. My name is Suzi Gablik."

"You're Suzi Gablik?" Joan's voice now chimed back in well-matched astonishment. "But I've always wanted to meet you!" It was as if two live wires had touched each other. And in that intoxicating moment of synchronicity, my secret prayer to be warmly received by this complete stranger was unexpectedly answered. "When we try to pick anything out by itself," the naturalist John Muir observed once, "we find it hitched to everything else in the universe."

Descriptions of Joan Halifax's accomplishments read like a prose locomotive: medical anthropologist, scholar, healer, ceremonialist, visionary, teacher, ordained Buddhist priest, deep ecologist, shaman. She is the author of several books on shamanism, as well as a spiritual autobiography, *The Fruitful Darkness*. The Ojai Foundation, an educational community that combines Buddhist practice, shamanism, Native American teachings, and wilderness living, is essentially her creation. For the twelve years she lived there, her vitality and charisma held the whole thing together.

Joan suggested that the best way to get to know her would be to take one of her journeys. Before long I found myself camping in the red rock deserts of the Southwest, hiking through sagebrush, and sheltering against canyon walls. Several times I spent long nights alone, fasting and praying in the tradition of the Native American vision quest, "crying for a vision" in some ancient pueblo ruin far from the industrial world. The experience affected me profoundly. I was not accustomed to living outside for days on end in the raw wind, sleeping on the ground in the dark with a sleeping bag pulled tightly over my head. In some ways it was a painful undertaking, but this was precisely the whole point: in this Pre-Cambrian landscape, my soul was being scoured. I was learning a new metaphysics: the erotic energy of nature, the philosophy of interdependence, the web of mutuality, how all phenomena are interconnected, a new ecological order of things. These were Joan's teachings, a powerful antidote to the modern "urban effect" of alienation from nature. In the silence at midnight, I couldn't always tell if I was making progress, but I was awakening to my ecological self.

TWENTY

I don't think I ever could have responded in the same way to a solemnly bearded guru in some faraway ashram, or to the fork-tongued Yaqui sorcerer who jolted Carlos Castaneda out of his common-sense perceptions and introduced him to the magical world of shamanism. Joan, on the other hand, was the perfect teacher for me. I was drawn to the romantic part of her, and to the ease with which she combined sophisticated worldliness with spiritual refinement. Her spirit was equally at ease conducting group meditations in a temple ruin in Chichén Itzá or floating loose in a local bar, laughing and drinking margaritas. Although a decade younger than me, she personified what I aspire to: strong womanhood and powerful convictions. The training I received from her in fierce compassion, deep ecology, and reverence for the earth changed my entire life orientation.

I didn't drop the magic ball once it had been handed to me. I went on to shed even more of my Western baggage and used all that I had learned to write *The Reenchantment of Art*. "The great collective project has, in fact, presented itself," I wrote, echoing Thomas Berry. "It is that of saving the earth." The book was a work-in-progress during many of the years I was teaching. "What does it mean to be a 'successful' artist working in the world today?" I asked my students, searching for answers that were above and beyond received notions.

The times were provocative and the art world, during the 1980s, was in great ferment. In my travels, I met many artists who were making big changes in their thinking. Like the individuals Ferguson had written about, they had stepped outside the dominant framework and were no longer pursuing the conventional vision of brisk sales, well-patronized galleries, and good reviews. Tired of isolation and disengagement, they wanted to make art "as if the world mattered," putting the emphasis of their work on cultivating a purposeful relationship with society, or on saving the environment, rather than on making a success in the art world. As I saw it, *The Reenchantment of Art* was giving voice to what was "in the air," and what was in the air was a new understanding of the nature of art. The notion of art as a private individual quest devoid of larger social and environmental concerns no longer seemed inspired.

Thinking of art as improvised collaboration or *relational* activity is an outrageous idea to those who grew up with the myth of individualism and self-expression as the signal of art's worth. Often, in my lectures, I would talk about the feminine qualities of receptivity and responsiveness, describing artists who were openly exploring the value of the feminine principle in their work, weaving together individual and community through a process of "deep listening," and opening up space to let groups that had been previously excluded speak directly of their own experience.

Ours is "doing" culture, however, which means that there is unrelenting pressure to produce, and to produce something visible, or you will get left behind. It is impossible to find oneself listening to others without the construction of a new kind of self, in which the ego is willing to take a back seat. In a fast-track culture, that is against all the rules. One event in particular brought home to me just how difficult it is for many people to face the implications of the new world view.

On this occasion, I was invited to share the lecture podium in Madison, Wisconsin with Hilton Kramer, for many years the lead art critic of the *New York Times*, well-known for his corrosive but conservative views.

I had to talk first. I blinked into the darkened auditorium and asked, "Are there viable alternatives to viewing the self in an individualistic manner? Can making art include more than just ourselves? Can art build community?" I could sense my questions were like gigantic, harrowing waves breaking on the beach of everyone's inherited experience. "To see our interdependence and our interconnectedness is the feminine perspective that has been missing, not only in our scientific thinking and policy-making, but in our aesthetic philosophy as well," I stated. I went on to give examples of "interactionism"—the intertwining of self and other—that essentially embodies the feminine approach for me, describing the first piece of art Mierle Laderman Ukeles did after she became the self-appointed artist-in-residence at the New York Department of Sanitation. It was a ritual performance work that took place over eleven months, in which she formally shook hands with 8,500 sanitation workers, facing each one and stating, "Thank you for keeping New York City alive." Ukeles considers that the real artwork is the handshake itself. "When I shake hands with a sanitation man," she says, "I present this idea and performance to them, and then, in how they respond, they finish the art." This piece has always been a favorite of mine, in part because it lets drop the unwieldy, autocratic personality of the modern artist-hero.

When I finished my talk, Kramer could hardly wait to turn the hose on me. "Shaking hands with sanitation workers has nothing to do with making art," he bellowed, as if a demon had got loose inside the room. "Solutions to social or environmental problems will never take place in an art gallery," because, he continued, "the only problems art can solve are aesthetic ones." It was as if I were back in that seminar room with Robert Motherwell, only seeing it all now through a glass darkly. Both of us were visibly choking on our own high-mindedness, determined to incriminate the other.

I have to confess, I'm more laid back these days. All that fever pitch, the need to be right, the din of overblown ideologies, seems like an hallucination now. At any rate, I have found my new religion: it is the whole world. As Rilke said, "I want to be with those who know secret things, or else alone."

Twenty-one

SEVERAL months ago, around ten o'clock in the evening, a gigantic delivery truck lumbered up my driveway and deposited on my porch eighteen collage paintings that had been sitting in storage for several decades with my dealer, Terry Dintenfass, in New York. I haven't painted or exhibited my work, or even seen any of these paintings, since my last exhibition more than twenty years ago. For all I knew, they could have rusted away in the warehouse, given my lack of concern about their fate during all these years.

For a long time I alternated, like a farmer tending different crops, between painting and writing. But after the publication of *Has Modernism Failed?*, writing seemed to come with an advantage that painting didn't: it offered me a voice. More than that, it put me full swing into the world, and turned my life to good account, making me feel useful. I began to prize the high adventure of sneaking around the world to get educated. At a certain point, therefore, I simply bailed out of being an artist and threw myself into being a writer. It didn't happen because of doubt or disloyalty or feelings of failure, but was rather a choice into which I settled quite easily.

Seeing the paintings again after such a long time, I am struck by how much my intuitive creative process led me, even before I ever read a single word of eco-philosophy or chaos theory, to seeing the world as a mutually interactive set of patterns in which everything is harmonically related to everything else. It was as if, without any instruction, I intuitively understood the implicate order enfolded within the Dionysian flux of nature. This kind of pattern-seeking—noticing the way seemingly disconnected elements fit together into a systemic whole—seems like it is hardwired into my brain and is alive in every aspect of what I do. It is a feeling for the relationship *between* things.

This is particularly visible in the last group of collages I made, a series of six paintings called *The Tangled Bank* (a phrase derived from Darwin's description of the wild profusion of forms in nature). Hidden congruities and formal affinities abound—the "morphic resonance," say, between a brain coral and a morel mushroom, or the optical symmetry between striped snakes, striped butterflies, and swarms of love-mad striped bees. This sense of a continuous metamorphic chain made up of tentacular creatures, coral tubers, sea anemones, human intestines, fossilized flowers, crawling slugs, jellyfish, crabs, plankton, shrimp, and larvae reminded me of the sinuous, tangled skeins in the "allover" canvases of Jackson Pollock, except that in my case, the images were never abstract. The work literally bristles with optical symmetries.

The early collages, by contrast, are more surrealistically anecdotal. They fabricate luxurious narratives that seem to go nowhere, composed from weird juxtapositions and disconcerting encounters. In the 1970s, I was into menace, murky happenings, distant sidelines, precarious grassy gorges, huge barren landscapes, smoke and fog, raging waterfalls, and exotic volcanoes—all of it congealing into what John Russell once called "the poetics of meaningful panic."

Sometimes I thought of myself as a movie director, working with an unorthodox set of stills. I liked using black and white images for their cinematic effect. One painting, from 1964, called *Movie*, inhabits a strange psychic zone in which a group of Nazi soldiers loiter beside a melted glacier where two polar bears are swimming.

A few of the early collages deliberately conjure up the mood and tone, the existential disquiet, encountered in the films of Michelangelo Antonioni. I was particularly fascinated by Antonioni's film, *L'Avventura*, a spasmodic study in futility and noncommunication. I can still remember the way the camera would pause endlessly on the back of Monica Vitti's voluptuous hair, as though it were part of a painting, or a pile of dead brown leaves pushed against a wall. One day, after a quarrel with her lover, Vitti takes off and disappears off the coast of Sicily. She is never found.

For some reason, the movie had a strange effect on me. It seemed to galvanize some kind of primitive fascination with disappearance. I was still in my twenties and, improbable as it sounds, I decided to take myself to Sicily on a lunatic pursuit: I wanted to break loose from the trappings of my known identity and simply vanish for a while in a place where I knew nobody, and nobody knew me. The plan was pretty mindless as plans go—live like a local, sip wine in cafés, flit around the ancient ruins, and dissolve into sun-browned anonymity. All my friends in New York warned me not to do it. A woman alone in Sicily, they said, was asking for trouble. I thought I could take care of myself, so I didn't listen. Instead, I found a boat in Brindisi that went to the coastal town of Siracusa. I landed in Sicily one bright and sunny Easter morning.

While on the boat, I struck up an acquaintance with a rather attractive man, who was part English and part Italian, and who turned out to be the police chief of Malta. Malta was where our boat was headed on the following day, and he was on his way home. Since the boat would be docked in Siracusa for the whole day, he offered to take me sightseeing. It seemed like an inauspicious beginning for my anonymity business, but I figured I could postpone for one day, without side-slipping too much from my proposed course.

We dropped anchor in Siracusa at dawn. I had no room reservation, just a list of tourist hotels in my pocket, and a rather bulky blue suitcase.

As it was Easter, all the hotels were completely full. For the first time since I'd left home, a vague sense of fear perforated my consciousness. In the very last hotel on my list, the desk clerk made a phone call, responding perhaps to my visible desperation, after which he wrote down an address on a piece of paper.

"You can try this place," he said. "The hotel is still under construction, but maybe they'll let you stay there."

When we arrived at the unfinished building, it was deserted. Then, seemingly from out of nowhere, a bandy-legged man with wall-eyes and glasses who bore a freakish resemblance to Jean-Paul Sartre, appeared and greeted us. Apologizing for the layer of plaster dust on the floor, he offered me a bargain price for the room and gave me a key. After locking my suitcase in the room, the police chief and I went out to explore the hills.

I can't remember a whole lot of what we did that day, but I do have a clear memory of sitting in the sloping ruins of an old amphitheater under a cornflower blue sky, and feeling immensely grateful for my new friend's reassuring presence. The odd thing was that all day long, he seemed determined to get me to leave Siracusa, return to the boat with him, and go to Malta. But I was adamant about going through with my bizarre plan, and resisted his urgings.

Whatever inner resolve I had began to crumple badly, however, as the afternoon light subsided, and I realized I would soon be alone in that deserted hotel, staring at my nose. My sense of being in the midst of nowhere suddenly intensified.

We began to wend our way back to the hotel, stopping briefly at a small café for something to eat. The waitress started up a conversation in Italian with my friend, and at one point, looking sideways at me, she inquired where we were staying. It was obvious she thought we were lovers.

My friend explained that he would be leaving shortly for Malta on the boat, but that I was staying on. Then he described the hotel to her.

I watched with horror as the blood drained from her cheeks and her eyes went dark. Then she said, "If you love this woman, don't let her stay there."

No need for further discussion. A single thought came to me, spare and staccato, as I looked at her face: *You are going to Malta tonight.* I didn't know what, but something, I could tell, was terribly wrong. The little café, which only a moment before had seemed so easy and friendly, was now charged with menace, as the waitress went on to explain that the bandy-legged man with the key, to all appearances an ordinary hotel manager, was in fact a well-known Sicilian criminal, who had been jailed more than once, in Sicily and in America, for crimes connected with the white-slave trade.

Totally panicked by now, I was ready to beeline it for the hotel, grab my bag, and head for the boat. I was running for my life, but my companion on the other hand, became like a hound on the scent. He wanted to go straight to the police station. There was a ferocity in the reckless abandon he was suddenly showing to pursue this. I didn't know it then, but his good name and reputation were on the line—in Malta, he was well-known for snuffing out racketeer ventures in female flesh. Called now by his ruling passion, my white knight was not to be persuaded away, but leapt on his charger instead.

The officer at the police station greeted us as if some cartoon figures had inadvertently come to life in the neighborhood. That is—until my friend exposed the annunciatory flash of a cop badge under his lapel, upon which he was led into a back room somewhere, while I was left behind in a chair, like a crumpled hanky. He emerged about twenty minutes later, and informed me that the police had suggested not spending a night in that hotel. A call was put through to the manager, stating that we were on the way, and should be allowed to leave without any fuss.

By night, the "empty" hotel, when we got there, was palpitating with action. Several rough-looking men were hurrying down the stairs as we came in. One was zipping up his fly. Doors slammed up above, and I saw a woman with a white towel wrapped around her naked body scuttle into the bathroom. It was obvious that, at night, the place was a lively bordello. It was also obvious that the police were in cahoots and knew exactly what was going on.

What might have befallen me had I spent the night there is hard to know, because I never made it to the finish line. But the situation was heavy with possibilities. My curious gusto for disappearing off the coast of Sicily like Monica Vitti might well have achieved its goal. Only when I was safely back on the boat to Malta and into the cocktail hour, did I begin to sag at the knees from the dangerous reality of what might have happened.

I ended up staying in Malta for three weeks, but I never really saw my policeman again. It wasn't until years later that I came to realize that this "random" coincidence—in which I had been thrown together synchronistically for a single day with the right person at the right time—may have been an angelic intervention that probably saved my life.

One never expects the wild card, yet in a canny way, it always seems to be there. I was reminded of this, thinking of my collages, and the way synchronicity would inevitably fling itself into the creative process in the final moments and bring all the diverse elements into alignment. There was always a point, a typical moment in the making of a collage, when I would find myself stymied. Some islet of canvas still remained bare, and defied completion. I would dive into my photo archive, hoping to weed out the last crucial piece—to no avail. My search would yield nothing, and there didn't seem to be any way to finish off the picture. Then I would wander along to some bookstore and just there, over to the right, would be exactly what was needed. It happened over and over again: the required image would appear synchronistically as if in response to my need. No painting was ever left in limbo, unfinished. Thinking about this now is a tonic reminder that, whether in life or in art, mysterious forces seem to guide the process. Events may appear random or unconnected, but a hidden order is at work beneath the surface in how it all comes together.

Twenty-two

THERE aren't too many friends I can talk to about my situation with Tom who aren't dubious. Most people think I'm on the swampy ground of a great meandering delta, and that I'll be left out in no-man's-land holding an empty bag. Surely anyone on top of the situation would have had the ending under control by now, airtight and guaranteed? As I proceed along the path, however, something is compelling me to stick it out in spite of everything. But clearly, getting to the other side is asking more of me than I ever bargained for. And I'm never really certain in my own mind that I haven't made a terrible mistake.

"What if the enterprise that you seek to develop is . . . now deadlocked because…you have your hand on a door that you insist upon opening that will go nowhere?" writes Gary Zukav in *The Seat of the Soul*. Treading water and marking time for so long now, I really feel the knife-edge of that comment in quite visceral ways. A *New Yorker* cartoon nails the feeling perfectly. Two Zen monks in robes and shaved heads are sitting side by side cross-legged on the floor. The younger one is looking somewhat quizzically at the older one, who is turned toward him and saying: "Nothing happens next. This is it."

In my heart I cherish the notion that fate has something remarkable in store. But the script I have in my head seems to be very much at odds with what is actually happening, and whenever I try to imagine how things will turn out, I feel like the White Queen in *Alice in Wonderland*, who practiced believing six impossible things before breakfast. I'm not interested in some botched encounter with interesting side effects. I am ruthless in my desire for a miracle, something perhaps with a biblical cadence, like Jesus producing wine out of water or a coin out of a fish's mouth. I want a showstopping finale: a clear lunar moment of fulfillment when the closed door finally opens and all the lights come on. In my heart, I want an outcome so glorious it will bring a whole world view based on rationalism to heel.

Sometimes it seems like it could happen, sometimes it doesn't. Much of the time, it feels as if I am on a train going nowhere. One day, in confusion, I write a letter to my friend Michael Grosso about my predicament. Michael is a sensitive and reliable expert in the psychodynamics of the paranormal. In his writing, he has blazed many new trails into psychic and spiritual realms, exploring everything from what makes people psychic to apparitions of Jesus's face on a tortilla. Whether it is afterlife research, out-of-body experiences, table-tilting or telepathy, Michael is a fount of knowledge. If anyone could offer me an open-minded perspective, it was him.

"In the greatest love stories," he writes me back, "even when the consummation is tragic, the heart is lifted and the poetry touches us. It's all in the telling, isn't it? No matter how your story ends, it can only succeed."

Although intended to console and reassure, this wasn't what I was hoping to hear. I had been hoping for a more full-bodied championing of my oracular transmissions, which I realize, challenge every personal, cultural, and relationship trope. Michael might, but I couldn't, go along with being so divinely indifferent to results.

"One's efforts are salutary and indispensable, but without results, they amount to nothing," warns the narrator in Paulo Coehlo's novel *The Pilgrimage*. Results count. Failure is not OK with me, although I knew it was a dark object I couldn't just ignore. Perhaps that was why I kept on reassessing my situation with the *I Ching*.

"Do not be afraid of any existing imbalance," it was telling me now. "There are secret forces leading together those who belong together. Do not allow yourself to be roused to anger by the seeming lack of progress."

TWENTY-TWO

This ability to tune in feels like a gift of spirit. Whenever I consult the *I Ching*, it's as if I am stepping into the current of divine will. Again and again I have the experience of distressing irresolution being suddenly displaced by a quasi-miraculous determination. My sense of futility disappears, and waiting seems plausible again, as if another time-release capsule has been inserted into my brain. But even with today's reading ringing forcefully in my ears, I still find myself wondering how much longer I can float down the Nile like Moses did, doing nothing more than lying in his basket.

In an oracular worldview, divination is not a strange or embarrassing activity. Many people today look down on it as "magical thinking," but the Dalai Lama believes in omens and oracles, and even Benjamin Franklin is said to have studied the Tarot. I remember reading that Jung used to feel as if a live intelligence was communicating with him when he used the *I Ching*. And now there is the provocative case of Neale Donald Walsch, who wrote the bestseller *Conversations with God*.

When his life in southern Oregon was going badly, Walsch wrote out a series of questions addressed to God, only to find that God began communicating with him through a "voiceless voice" inside his head. I think Walsch's experiences inhabit the same terra incognita as my own. Are his conversations actual talks with God? Is it possible to talk with God? Or is it just a fantasy, invented to make life more interesting, excite our admiration, and make some money? Walsch believes the conversations are real.

Some people have described opening the Bible and getting direct hits when they ask it to tell them something they want to know. Elisabeth Kübler-Ross claims she can write down questions with her right hand and get the answers with her left. Walsch is informed by God that his answers may appear anywhere—in the next song he hears, or in the information from the next article he reads, or in the chance utterance of the next person he meets. "So go ahead now," God says to Walsch in the book. "Ask me anything. Anything. I will contrive to bring you the answer. The whole universe will I use to do this. So be on the lookout . . ."

Would this work for me, too, if I threw out a question? I decide to experiment. "What is the reason Tom has left his encyclopedia of Chinese medicine with me?"

I open up the dictionary at random and let my finger drop where it will on the page. It falls directly on the word "proclaim"—to declare, announce officially, put on the map, communicate, state with conviction. When I look up "proclaim" in the thesaurus, it offers, in addition, "to pledge, promise, vow, commit oneself."

One person's synchronistic experiences may not be all that convincing to someone else, but in this case, the correlation with my own obscure intuition is both unexpected and striking. The answer rings true.

The next day, I am drawn to try the same procedure again. I want to know whether, given the emotional distance and resistance, Tom is really interested in this relationship. My finger falls onto a descriptive passage under the word "mine": to tunnel underground, to proceed secretly, below the surface, undercover.

The sense of proceeding secretly, and out of sight, conveyed to me the spiritual essence of Tom: a certain kind of man who, when going through a dark phase of internal transformation, will not show his struggle outwardly but remains hidden and opaque until he has settled things within himself. In fact, the image of tunneling underground, like a root system you never see that burrows its way beneath the earth, was one that had already made an indelible impression on my psyche, since it is a symbol for initiatic journeys. The dark tunnel has long been a feature of initiation rites; initiates had to crawl on their bellies through specially constructed underground tunnels and surrender to an incubation in the darkness, before finally experiencing a rebirth. Reading the symbol, I take the measure of my own situation. Was there really a parallel here, or was I just making something out of nothing?

Several days pass, and I am wondering if my bizarre oracle can assert itself even against the impediments of confusion and delay. I decide to risk the essential question, "Will he ever take the step into partnership?" When I dip into the dictionary this time, my finger falls on the word "court," whose meaning, as a verb, is "to pay attention to, to woo, to solicit, to seek."

The answer isn't at all what I was expecting, and it produces in me a kind of primordial anxiety, of the sort one might feel looking at the burning bush. Some part of me, I realize, is expecting an arrow through the heart, afraid of the sting of betrayal. Sometimes, my fascination with divining is the only thing which keeps me, still as a statue, in front of this Berlin Wall.

Suddenly I understand why people prefer to discredit oracular consciousness—why they resist the idea of accessing information that exceeds the boundaries of normal, everyday intelligence. This was no parlor game I was in. It takes a gambler's heart to trust one's guidance to prove itself. What if I am setting myself up for a fall? Divination, I realized, could only take me so far. After that, a leap of faith is required.

If some things in life were simple, this obviously was not. For the first time I began to see why conventional wisdom in our culture is so skeptical about psi phenomena and eager to dismiss it as unreliable. Faced with such mystical manifestations, is one meant to believe the future is already formed and just waiting to be revealed? The mind swaggers and balks at the mere possibility of this. Is it possible that we do not, in some sense, decide or choose things, but that life lives us just as much as we live life?

Despite the tangible feeling of revelation I had experienced, despite the sense of reassurance and comfort that seems to have come from beyond, I still didn't know whether to trust my guidance, or whether all this was some self-serving fantasy I had made up. The whole thing was like a maze that doubles and doubles on itself, but far more confusing.

When two interfering perceptions of reality clash with each other, it's hard to know which of them is really the truth. That's the spiritual test in all our lives, according to the medical intuitive, Caroline Myss. "Act on your inner guidance," she states in *Anatomy of the Spirit*, "and give up your need for 'proof' that your inner guidance is authentic. The more you ask for proof, the less likely you are to receive any . . . Learn to trust what you cannot see far more than what you can see."

We live in the aftermath of the Age of Enlightenment, an age of reason, and of "facts." Not until we can grasp a little of the working of the ancient mind can we even begin to appreciate the "magic" of the world they lived in. The ancients could receive revelations all the time; in fact, receiving oracular messages has been a time-honored tradition in just about every civilization except ours. Oracle temples were well-known in Egyptian and Mediterranean antiquity, and were consulted frequently, for concerns as diverse as property, crops, and health, as well as more complex affairs of state, elections, or war. In Greece, for example, at the temple of Dodona, a talking oak tree would produce answers. A priestess would listen to the rustling leaves and pronounce the words she heard. In these cultures, people believed there are two sides to existence—the side you see and the side you don't see—and they traveled from far and wide in order to receive oracular revelations from invisible forces they believed were behind everything in life. Usually these revelations were delivered through the medium of questions and answers.

Other cultures practiced divination with oracle bones, animal entrails, or tortoise shells. In his book *Synchronicity: The Bridge Between Matter and Mind*, F. David Peat describes how the Shang people, who lived in China during the Bronze Age, consulted tortoise shells, and through the ritual of reading cracks on the shell, were able to organize and maintain their whole culture. Peat argues that their worldview cannot be dismissed as the aberration of a backward and obscure people, since the Shang are considered as one of the world's major early civilizations. Their culture survived for a period longer than that of the British Empire, and their synchronistic world view lasted longer than post-Renaissance science has existed.

If divination counted as a sacred art in many cultures, and

TWENTY-TWO

people's lives intertwined with these practices in familiar ways, in Western culture today, most of us live without access to this visionary part of the psyche—unless we happen to have developed our own techniques for getting over the edge of ordinary consciousness. But what happens, in our present civilization, when you ask for a sign and then get it—when the veil is lifted and the answer comes? Suspicion. Intense suspicion. The habit of rationality has conditioned us cruelly in this regard, by crippling our responses. Instead, our skepticism demands to know the source of these messages, and like me, wonders if they are reliable. I had just experienced a meaningful cluster of oracular revelations. But were they, I wondered, really orchestrated by a divine source? I decide to plunge even further into the belly of the beast—and ask.

"Where are these messages coming from?" This time, I plumb the depths using *The Book of Runes*, an ancient Viking oracle that has been modernized by Ralph Blum and is commonly available in bookstores. Reaching my hand into the wine-colored bag, I pull out a rune and get "Ansuz," the Messenger Rune, whose keynote is *receiving*: messages, signals, gifts. When the Messenger Rune brings sacred knowledge, it says, one is truly blessed. And then I feel the sharpness of these words like hot sealing wax. "Drawing this Rune tells you: connection with the Divine is at hand."

Tears run down my cheeks. Twentieth-century science assures us there is no one out there, but somehow, in all our urban-professional expertise, we may have missed the real structure and meaning of the world. Or, more precisely, we have let the fire die in the engine. We think we understand, but our tilted vision has a hard time recognizing what the great Sufi mystic and poet Jelaluddin Rumi saw with ease: "There is someone who looks after us / From behind the curtain." We can only see that light reflected in a smoky mirror.

In her book about the Dark Goddess, *Dancing in the Flames*, Marion Woodman describes an intense, revelatory moment when she encountered the divine presence in her own life, and it shattered the smoky mirror. She describes her chronic suffering from a loud ringing in her ear (tinnitus), a condition resulting from a car accident, which occurred in 1968. Two years after surgery, it was still driving her crazy, but the doctors told her there was no cure.

On one particular agonizing night, she found herself praying to God to take away the ringing in her ear or to let her die. Then a mock-orange bush in full bloom appeared from out of nowhere, floating spectacularly in the charged silence. It was made palpable by the heavy perfume. The sweetness, she states, "moved into every cell of my body until the perfume and I were one." The vision was utterly enthralling, and after it faded, the ringing in her ear ceased. It never returned. Woodman claims that the incident shattered the world as she had known it and changed her life forever.

Profound psychic experience alters us. Nothing else gives such a direct, convincing sense of the divine. I could see that I had to accept my enrollment in some kind of spiritual adventure that might not, for the time being, be entirely intelligible. No authentic initiatory process begins in the certainty of its outcome. Letting it all happen just as it needs to, not taking matters into my own hands—well, I was still trying to learn how to do it.

With this in mind, I settle myself in a chair before my altar. Not forcing things, allowing the mystery to ripen in me, is itself a spiritual task. One of the great Taoist secrets is that emotional excess and striving from the ego will immediately bring you down. Hidden small endeavors, on the other hand, regulate the deepest and most transcendent layer of inner life.

Reaching into my votive box, I remove two strands of the beautiful gold ribbon I had earlier severed. I knot them back together again at each end and create a symbolic circle. It is my way of reconnecting the relational loop. Then I ask my oracle to speak one more time.

"Will I ever succeed in having this union with Tom?" I open the book and let my spinner finger fall. It lands, like a horseshoe on a peg, directly on the word "avowed": affirmed, confirmed, guaranteed, promised, sworn by all that is holy.

That night, the *I Ching*, my prophet in yellow cloth, adds a final word. "The ridgepole is braced. You have succeeded in becoming a master of the situation. Any use of it for ulterior motives or personal success will be humiliating."

Twenty-three

BROWSING recently in my local bookstore, I discovered, on one of the art shelves, a newly published collection of essays by the art critic Eleanor Heartney. In one of the essays, Heartney starts off by wondering what has gotten into art critics these days. None of them, she implies, are up to snuff anymore. What was once a passionate enterprise has turned into a surly, sullen kind of indifference.

Positioning herself as a sort of friendly, watchful owl, she observes this disrepair in the ranks and launches into her critique of various writers. Barbara Rose, for instance, complains on her high horse about the deterioration of high art into philistinism, but writes regularly for a fashion magazine. At the other extreme, Hal Foster and Douglas Crimp, theorists of aesthetic philosophy, bore the reader to death, she claims, with "readerproof" essays on deconstruction. Discreetly wedged between these diagnostic impeachments is a brief reference to me: "Suzi Gablik turns mystic."

A comment like this, with no follow-up, brands you. It has the embarrassing thrust of "gone fishin'," or "disappeared into the Rembrandt darkness." It leaves its black mark.

Jungian therapist Helen Luke has written eloquently about the difficulties, in patriarchal culture, of investing energy in the interior psyche. A life not devoted to outward accomplishment suffers a loss of prestige—but this loss must be endured as an essential ingredient of the soul's journey. A conscious and painful sacrifice is necessary, even if it is not recognized by others.

A postcard arrives in the mail from a friend. She wants to know how my "mystical" relationship is going. Rightly or wrongly, I sense disparagement in my friend's question—"mystical" in this case being a code word for: Are you still in that hopeless situation?

Mysticism, I write back in my *agent provocateur* mood, is hardly the point. A plain-sailing relationship would have been great, with Superman wrapping me in great rectangles of love, but it's not what's happening. My "mystical" relationship feels more like commando training, with all the harrowing aspects of being made to tackle difficult tasks like cascading down cliffs on my back and eating barbed wire for breakfast. It's a bit like parachuting behind enemy lines when you can't see what is on the other side and the energies of the moment are against you. But in a weird way, I like it. Paradoxically my encounter with the "rough warrior" archetype is forcing me beyond my secure boundaries. The experience is creating a self permeated with resolve, tenacity, constancy, and grit. None of this would have happened if things had gone smoothly, if I hadn't been blown off course for awhile. And since I'm using the situation as an opportunity to explore my own spiritual potential, even if the task is futile, I have to fulfill it.

In *The Writing Life*, Annie Dillard asks a painter friend, who lives in a cabin on the beach on one of the San Juan Islands, how his work is going. "Feels like I'm about in the middle of the channel now," he finally responds. "I just keep hoping the tide will turn and bring me in."

If I have learned anything so far on this journey, it is perhaps that the world really does function by rules other than those I had previously assumed. Unpredictable forces and factors operate behind the scenes that bring solutions we can't foresee because they come from deeper spiritual sources. Living the magical life means receiving continuous feedback from one's ambient situation; it can be triggered from every direction. In the great cosmic drama, the magic is always there, if you are open to it. So even if the responses we desire from the present are not forthcoming, we can never know in advance how things will go. There is always a hidden ace-up-the-sleeve.

"When there's a big disappointment, " Pema Chödron writes, "we don't know if that's the end of the story. It may just be the beginning of a great adventure." Many years ago, when John Russell and I were courting, in the eleventh hour everything just came to pieces. John had made the decision to leave his wife and live with me. On the appointed day, however, an altogether different scenario materialized, and instead of John, a letter appeared in my mailbox, which attempted to explain to me the impossibility of carrying out the plan. It seemed that in the effort of uprooting his marriage, some component of self-assurance had failed him. The agony was framed in a single sentence of articulate forlornness I shall never forget; it was, he said, like trying to cut down an oak tree with a pen knife. I was aghast, shaken to the core, a shifting blur of pain. And I didn't know what to do.

Today, I'd probably take my cue from Kate Vaiden, a fictional character in a novel by Reynolds Price, and follow her no-nonsense advice: "Strength just comes in one brand—you stand up at sunrise and meet what they send you and keep your hair combed." But then, when I saw that my ship had wrecked, I wanted revenge. I planned to gather all of John's letters and presents to me in a box and mail them to his wife. I probably would have done it, except that the psychiatrist I went to see when the catastrophe struck was so outraged by my plan she threatened to cancel my therapy if I tried to go through with it.

Months passed, miserable shell-shocked months, in which I had no more contact with John. Then one day I went to an art gallery on Bond Street, and there he was, staring docilely at a Ben Nicholson painting. I think we both experienced a feeling of shock—but centuries of civilization notwithstanding, there wasn't even a conversation between us. John scuttled off embarrassed into another room, pretending he hadn't seen me. In an interesting onrush of emotion, it was as if he suddenly became Hitler, Stalin, and

Mussolini all rolled up into one—and I wanted to kill him.

Exactly what happened after that is a little bit fuzzy in my mind, but it went something like this. Either I wrote John a letter, in which I denounced his baboonish flight, or I just thought about writing it. Whichever it was, an affectionate apology arrived soon after in the mail. It was then that fate did one of those incredible flip-flops worthy of the circus acrobats of China, and the incident that had been so disappointing became the stepping-stone that drew us back together again and gave us another chance. After that, John really did leave his marriage behind, and we were able to unite.

If I reflect on my life so far, I know that it's really true: something unforeseen will always change everything. Life is a road that sneaks past all the maps. And yet it all fits together as neatly as a crossword puzzle.

Still, the question persists. Are we the authors of our fate? Or are we at the mercy of the tides?

In one of his many conversations with God, God says to Neale Donald Walsch: "Your own life is the way it is because of *you*, and the choices you have made—or failed to make." Obviously the will to persevere in an unrewarding course plays a crucial role in the attainment of our goals. The choice to push or not push ourselves in a matter is the mark of the courageous life, and has a causal power in the world. I remember, for instance, at a Common Boundary Conference, hearing Sarah Ban Breathnach describe, in a keynote address, how her best-selling book *Simple Abundance* had been rejected thirty times by publishers in the space of two years—until one day all that failure and disappointment and rejection simply turned around on a dime.

In some sense we are indeed the authors of our fate, but in another, the opposite is also true: there is no choice, because we don't control anything. "Nobody does anything and nobody can do anything," P. D. Ouspensky writes in *In Search of the Miraculous*. "This is the first thing that must be understood. *Everything happens*."

TWENTY-THREE

The truth is we really have no idea why anything happens. A human being may simply be a cluster of particular forces magnetized, in any given moment, by a unique configuration of providence and grace. The ego and its will, the sense that we are in control of our fate, is only one half of the equation. There is something numinous at that point around which these two paradoxical forces interact and become one—a fusion point of almost impenetrable ambiguity and blur.

The elusive essence of what I'm talking about, the symbiotic relationship between will and grace, can show up in odd places. One day my friend Othello Anderson, who lives in Chicago, took his small daughter kite-flying in Lincoln Park. It was a clear, blustery October day. The kite wrenched around in a powerful gust of wind and became trapped high up in a tree. The child was inconsolable.

Unfazed, my friend decided to coax the kite down with his thoughts and passionate persistence. Standing directly under the tree, he peered up at the kite from below. Then, using all his will and concentration, he quietly merged his energy field with that of the kite, urging and encouraging it to come down. Bit by bit, in slow motion, dropping a little and then stalling again, the kite gradually descended far enough so that it could be lifted out of the tree. This commanding act of magical persuasion took about an hour and a half.

Twenty-four

IN 1988, the Yugoslavian performance artist Marina Abramovíc traveled to China in order to do a performance work that involved walking across the Great Wall. She and her partner/collaborator Ulay started walking towards each other from opposite ends of the Wall—a distance of 3,700 miles—and continued until they met, months later, somewhere in the middle.

Initially they had decided to call the piece *The Lovers: The Great Wall Walk*, and imagined they might even get married wherever it was along the wall that they found each other again. Instead, the event and its consequences were altered before transit, because the personal relationship between the two artists, who had been together for twelve years, shattered less than a year before starting their epic walk. But even though the personal bond between them was irrevocably broken, they decided to go through with their last work. After three months of walking the wall from opposite directions, the two artists finally came face-to-face on a stone bridge. They embraced, reversed, and with scalding dignity, left separately for Amsterdam.

Marina was on the road in China. And metaphorically speaking, I'm on the road at home. But something about her arduous and lonely walk, with its fateful currents, resonates with me. Hers was a journey without consolation. Marina knew exactly what to expect at the end of it: "I was confronted with just the bare wall and me. I had to rearrange my motivation," she declared at one point. Can I really expect a more satisfying conclusion to my own journey? Or will I need to rearrange my motivation, too?

If I look inside for an internal image that is guiding me, it would have to be that of Pythia sitting on her tripod, bestowing oracular powers and moments of illumination from the seam between the worlds. I keep asking the oracle over and over to remind myself, when I'm feeling lonely and exposed like Marina, that a hidden future may appear at any time, as if from nowhere, vivid and fully formed.

"Will there be union at the end of my walk?" Once again, I've thrown my interrogatory javelin at the thesaurus.

"Think, assume, believe, probable, likely, on the cards." Today there is something interesting in the air. Today I intend to ask a flotilla of questions, flatly, efficiently, in one big, collective wave.

"What is the meaning of this relationship?"

"Veracity, authenticity, realness, truth, the real McCoy, the real thing, not a fake, well thought out, well-grounded, unromantic, genuine, no other, true as steel, stand the test."

A slightly manic mood begins to overtake me. It's a bit like picking up radio waves from another dimension. "Then why does he show so little affection?"

"Redundant, inflation, superfluous, expendable, pampering, unnecessary, gilding the lily." I feel like a Zen master who has just hit the bulls-eye at sixty paces, without looking at arrow or target. "Then why does every step seem blocked? What keeps him from moving forward to embrace this?"

"House divided against itself, ambivalence, ineptitude, fish out of water, odd man out." By now, tears are streaming down my face again, so much does this answer correspond with my own inner sense of truth. "What bridges the gap, then?"

"Discovering, inspiration, influence, provocation, encouragement, planting, watering, cultivation, cooperation, destiny, fate." It's as if a strange and beneficial spell has been cast in response to my questions. "So what should I do?"

"Go wooing, pay court, speak fondly to, offer one's heart, dazzle, excite love, command respect, endearments, love tokens."

Ancient pueblo cliff dwellers living in the desert were able to call down rain whenever they needed it. The magician Houdini could produce cannonballs and bouquets from a hat. He could fill an empty silver punch bowl with steaming coffee. The Yoruba trickster-figure Eshu could make beads appear with a clap of his hands. And like a snake that sees its prey in infrared, I had just retrieved this potent information, clear and strong, about my whole predicament. Rarely have I felt such exhilaration—or such unmediated fear.

There is a special bun in the oven this week: the arrival in Blacksburg of Mary Caroline (M.C.) Richards—poet, potter, painter, teacher, author, philosopher, and artist. My first encounter with M.C. was in a summer study session I attended, during 1951, at Black Mountain College, an experimental, avant-garde school that flourished (1933–56) in the wilds of North Carolina and attracted many innovative thinkers, artists, poets, and musicians. I was just out of high school, and had never been away from home by myself. Black Mountain was my graduation present from parents who were unwilling to send me out of town to college where I would be, for four academic years, beyond their obsessions of control. The summer I went there, I was only sixteen.

Imprudent or incredibly naïve, my parents had no idea where they were sending me. They had never heard of the place, nor, for that matter, had I. I was allowed to go because another girl, who lived in the same apartment building as we did, was going, which meant that I wouldn't have to be alone.

The nonconformist atmosphere of the school proved to be quite challenging for us both, and when my friend's sinuses totally blocked up, she began to hate the place desperately. After a week of continuing misery, she left. I stayed. It was one of those defining choices in life. Although I was only there for two months, in that unorthodox environment, my maverick self, which was not easily accommodated at home, had the time and the provocation to emerge.

M.C. was just finishing her six-year stint on the faculty, where she taught English and made pottery. I remember finding her a bit intense—a flinty, exotic, and somewhat forbidding figure. I didn't see M.C. again for forty-five years. But in the 1960s, I read her books—*Centering* and *The Crossing Point*—on subjects so rich they weren't listed in the catalogues. "We are not meant to work for wages but for wholeness," she wrote in her forthright, authoritative voice. Then I encountered her again at a celebratory reunion for Black Mountain alumni held a few years ago on the site of the old campus, which is now a boy's summer camp. We discovered ourselves as kindred spirits and became good friends.

M.C. is in Blacksburg this week at the invitation of Ray Kass, a professor in the art department of Virginia Tech, who has invited her to conduct one of his well-known Mountain Lake Workshops, which will draw on her opulent talents to include a combination of pottery-making, poetry, and painting. It is being offered to students and a select group of local artists. What M.C. really teaches in her eloquent way is how to fulfill the promise of the moral life under late twentieth-century capitalism without capitulating to its ideologies, psychologies, or technologies, and without the gears of contagious selfishness bearing down.

At eighty-one years,* her beauty tempered somewhat by an exploding mane of white hair, M.C. dresses in the brightly colored, hand-embroidered Mexican shirts that I remember, with a rich heap of multi-textured necklaces terraced on her chest. Her youthful ebullience, spontaneity, and simplicity are still intact. I often imagine that if our culture were ever to have a durable tradition of "living national treasures" (like those, say, in Japan), M.C. would surely have to be counted among them. For years she has lived as a co-worker in a Rudolf Steiner Camphill Community, working with individuals who have developmental disabilities, teaching them pottery, and cooking dinner twice a week for the whole community.

That the greatest art is less the creating of things than the creating

---

* Sadly, M. C. Richards died on September 9, 1999 at the age of eighty-three.

TWENTY-FOUR

of our own life is a crucial notion M.C. and I share. But if the making of ourselves is the really true and living work of art, where, then, are the boundaries? Here is a potent and pliant dictum from one of her books that I particularly love: "Perhaps if I had a coat of arms, this would be my motto: weep and begin again."

M.C. arrives in her tan station wagon crammed full of paintings. On this, her third visit to Blacksburg, Ray has arranged for an exhibition of her work at the university art gallery. And while she is giving her workshop, I will be the flame-tender at home, absorbing tensions, serving up morning coffee with hot milk, and watching from the sidelines.

We visit for a while on my back deck, facing the sun, and drink a cup of tea. Conversation with M.C. is never trivial. We've only just begun to share the intimacy of each other's lives. Like me, M.C. has spent most of her life without a male partner. I've written to her about Tom, which has kindled an interest in meeting him. Tom, too, seems excited by the prospect of meeting M.C., after reading the books of hers which I have passed on to him.

The evening takes on a special intimate splendor as the two of them converse over dinner like two chips off the old block. Something clicks, even though M.C. has a rasping cough and isn't feeling well. Tom is at his best, like a tart, wild plum. His usual discomfort and standoffishness with people he doesn't know seems nonexistent.

The euphoria of the evening is enhanced when, after Tom leaves, M.C. affirms how much she enjoyed meeting him. He's a serious man, she says, and adds that she likes serious men. That they should have been so naturally taken with each other renews my optimism. I need to remember this when I come to the next impasse.

The following day, as we are having lunch, Tom arrives, unannounced, to bring a bottle of Chinese cough medicine for M.C. But he doesn't linger. We are, in any case, supposed to link up again later that afternoon at her opening, and for the poetry reading directly after that, to be held in a local bookstore across the street from the gallery.

The stardust moment turns to ash, however, when Tom fails to appear at either event. I feel my distress compounding at yet another piece of inexplicable behavior. Tom's tracks are just so hard to read. They point in all directions, so you are never sure which way to proceed. Sometimes it seems as if he is a twentieth-century version of those Cheyenne warriors I once read about, determined to create bafflement in their doings by making everything point the other way. With contrary logic, they would say "no" when they meant "yes," and "yes" when they meant "no." Even the covering of their lodge was inside out, and the smoke-hole was deliberately turned the wrong way. If sent away, they came nearer, and if asked to walk on foot, they would mount a horse. Tom, too, was like that, keeping clear of all the demands others might make of him.

When we get home that night, M.C. proposes telephoning Tom to find out why he didn't come. On the phone, he apologizes. He had laid down briefly for a nap, and inadvertently slept through it all.

True love and prayer, Thomas Merton once said, are learned in the hour when love becomes impossible and the heart is turned to stone. Tom might be labyrinthine in his ways, which sometimes required reading upside down, but he was the master of a disciplined practice, with far too many subtleties of intelligence to allow stupid or careless behavior of that order. However reasonable or straightforward his excuse seems to M.C., I'm doubtful. In my bones I feel his excuse is a dodge.

The Tibetans say disappointment is the swiftest chariot to enlightenment, but I can hardly contain mine. I try to remember all my spiritual teachings: You don't know everything. Nothing is wrong. Avoid getting trapped in your own reflexive reactions. Don't lash out. And don't bail out even when there's a big disappointment. "Weep and begin again." I remind myself of what Annie Dillard recommends for nightmare: "You eat wild carrot, which is Queen Anne's lace, or you chew the black seeds of the male peony." I try the oracle again.

"What do I do now?" An answer comes back that I'm not expecting. "Build up strength, replenish, rally, recover, come around."

Why me? I'm not in the mood to rally or come around. "What happens if I don't?" The answer doesn't pull any punches. "Trouble in paradise, regress, backslide, not maintain an improvement."

One could argue, I suppose, that my little oracle phenomenon is no more implausible than Sitting Bull listening to meadowlarks for advice. Usually, at these kinds of impasses, if I watched for road signs here and there, I could find the way forward without creating new traps, or having my nose flattened. But this time, I was finding it really hard not to make a negative interpretation.

"It only takes one negative interpretation," as James Redfield has pointed out, "to stop everything." And to give up on the whole process. Giving up cuts through disappointment like antacid cuts through a sour stomach. It was the ultimate concealed weapon, and I always carried it with me.

A few days later, I am looking through the notes in my notebook when a sentence, copied out months before from a book by Ken Wilber, nudges me like a gentle kick from under the table. "The question is," it says, "not does the map match the territory? But can the mapmaker be trusted?"

In the magical life, you have to take chance seriously. You have to recognize "lucky finds." You have to be alert, or the message may fly right by you. It's like a ball that won't wait. I immediately recognize this passage as meant for me in this moment. *Can the mapmaker be trusted?* When you find your trusted person, one of my oracles had told me, your mind will be at ease. But how could I guard against the danger of judging wrongly, perhaps even of following the wrong God home?

Twenty-five

YOU NEVER KNOW, with Tom, when he will show up or what he will do when he arrives, but one thing is certain: it takes a long time to earn his trust, and it would take only a moment to lose it. In his kind of equation, there would be no need of explanations, no desire to spell anything out. The Buddhas do not tell the way, it says somewhere in the *Dhammapada*; it is for you to swelter at the task. And you can't get there by asking questions. You have to trust the integrity of the mapmaker.

I understood that I had reached a point where it was necessary to move forward in faith or not move at all. Faith begins, if it begins at all, where knowledge leaves off. According to Gregg Levoy in *Callings*, certain thresholds cannot be crossed by way of reason or ambition. Dante and Virgil were not permitted to pass through one particular threshold of Inferno until they left reason and intellect behind.

Recently my friend Satish Kumar, the editor of *Resurgence* magazine, and his wife June, made a sacred pilgrimage around Mt. Kailash in Tibet, which they described as being excruciatingly difficult. Tibetans making this same journey will usually leave an article of clothing, or a drop of blood or hair, as part of leaving their prejudices and grievances behind. On approaching the summit, their Tibetan guide counseled them: "Leave your fear, your ego, your anxiety and your meanness here."

In the Philippines it is customary to carry a piece of the lover's clothing on one's person, which is believed to reinforce the relationship and mutual faithfulness. Sometimes in fairy tales, when the heroine finds herself at her lowest ebb, she will discover that her salvation can be effected through the influence of magical tokens that were in her possession all along.

Sitting on my Black Madonna altar is a pair of glittering red shoes, no bigger than a goldfish's fin—a miniature replica of Dorothy's wonder-working ruby slippers from *The Wizard of Oz*. In the story, the ruby slippers transport Dorothy on a magical journey and bring her good fortune on the road of trials. I had received them as a special gift from a friend, and part of their cachet resided in the fact that they are a possession I couldn't replace. Suddenly I am gripped by the thought of giving the red shoes to Tom. They will represent a choice to place the whole momentum of my being at the disposal of my story, and to come down on the side of adventure.

At the heart of my offering is a concealed vow: to always act out of loyalty. Wherever the path may lead—whether it goes in spirals or circles, and even if it is absurd—I will follow it. From now on, like Sisiphus, I will practice the higher fidelity that raises rocks.

I put the shoes into a tiny box. Then, a few days later, I deposit the box on top of Tom's royal blue nylon jacket, which is folded up on the floor in class. After warm-up stretches, I practice the Tai Chi sword form, concentrating hard so that my wrist will whip the sword around correctly, in a full-circle pinwheel turn.

How will this sassy little symbol be received? In my mind's eye I picture it like a ripe raspberry fallen between the swords on Tom's floor. The image shocks as much as it enlightens. Will my magical token be accepted and honored, or will it be ridiculed and dismissed?

"Daphne is wooden," Thomas Moore writes in *Original Self*. She doesn't want any kind of union. So when Apollo pursues her, she eludes him by turning herself into a tree. Daphne has no use for the sentimentality of relationship; she doesn't want to be loved or desired. According to Moore, she represents the part of us that doesn't want to be civilized, communicative, available, friendly, present, or articulate, but which instinctively flies from even the most noble of attentions, the most humane of admirers.

As soon as I read these words, they glow in the dark with a certain gruesome specificity. What if Tom really wasn't Eros at all, but Daphne? I'm still dragging my heels in no-man's-land. My little plot pirouette with the red shoes has not produced any visible results. Ever faithful to his solitary path, Tom does not seem to be reveling in the fact that life has at last sent him a soulmate and a declaration of love. In fact, except for class twice a week, I'd seen even less of him than usual. Without emotional coziness, I'm navigating the winter badly, battered by an intolerable accumulation of small hassles, a respiratory infection, and faulty wiring in the septic tank. Everything feels frozen and inflexible, stalemated and stuck.

Maybe triumph and reward ensue after great struggles, and maybe not, Gregg Levoy stubbornly reminds me. Sometimes what we hope for doesn't materialize and sometimes it does. His words do little to staunch my disappointment, and volatile emotions well up ominously from below as I head into town to meet a friend for lunch. But my friend doesn't appear, causing the shadows of my downcast mood to fill out even more.

A sudden flash of color casts a glow on the gloom when another friend appears out of nowhere and slips into the vacant seat opposite mine. My friend Dee Ann is a therapeutic social worker, who specializes in sand tray and mandala art therapy. Sand tray is an image system in which the client is offered a variety of provocative and colorful objects to choose from, and to create a story with, by arranging them in a shallow box filled with sand. Dee's office looks like an "Aladdin's cave" curio cabinet, brimming with hundreds of small, exhilarating objects arrayed on wall-to-wall shelves, each one radiating some kind of talismanic quality. When read metaphorically, the client's choice and arrangement of objects will often have reverberations of meaning that can aid the therapist in understanding the deeper issues at work in an individual's life.

Sensing my dejection, Dee lays a gallant hand on my arm, demanding to know what's wrong. Fortunately she is a close friend to whom I can bare my spirit when I'm feeling down. For a while she listens patiently while I blow off steam. Like Kierkegaard's "knight of infinite resignation," I'm afraid my long, drawn-out quest will not be fulfilled. I may have to give up on happy endings and long-held fantasies. And there won't be any prize for that.

Without warning, Dee stands up, as if ready to leave. "I found a present for you the other day," she says, "and I think I should give it to you right now. It's outside, in my car."

On returning, she puts something small in my hand, the way a priest might offer a Communion wafer. I can hardly believe my eyes when I find myself staring down at a beguiling pair of red shoes, identical to the ones I'd given away to Tom.

Not being indifferent to small iconic objects herself, Dee had been galvanized when she saw the red shoes on my altar. I could tell she viewed them as rocket fuel for her sand-tray collection, and I knew that I had whipped up some unwilling envy when I'd admitted that I'd given them away to Tom.

"Where on earth did you get these red shoes?" I ask, hardly able to contain my astonishment.

"At Kroger's," Dee replies, smiling.

"In the supermarket! How is that possible?" The idea strikes me as ludicrous. "I suppose you found them stashed somewhere between the laundry detergent and the breakfast cereal?" No bigger than a cashew nut, they would never even be seen.

Dee begins to describe how she found the red shoes. They were sitting on a shelf in a glass case near the video rental section of the store. It was almost like a mysterious apparition. A golden light seemed to draw her attention in the direction of the case as she was walking by, causing her to notice two pairs of tiny crimson shoes that were glistening among some small glass objects. Dee promptly bought both pairs.

I ask whether, if there had only been one pair, she would have given them to me or kept the shoes for herself. Kept them for herself, she says.

Suddenly I feel positive again. But it is yet another detail which actually convinces me that some breach of regular functioning must have been involved in the whole bizarre episode. Only after I am seated in my car, headed for home, and have turned on the ignition, do I realize that I have mistakenly gone to the wrong restaurant. Later I confirm that the friend I was supposed to have met for lunch that day was indeed waiting for me all along, but in another restaurant.

When we give ourselves as a gift to the life of the spirit, says Levoy, that life reciprocates. But we can't fake our sincerity. "The gods and our own souls know when we're being sincere and when we're just smiling and saying cheese," he writes.

Inevitably that initial spark, that satori-like split second in the light, vanishes, and its powerful effects begin to fade again. Revelatory experience comes and goes, spinning back out of view like a season or a moon, and then you have to wait a long time for it to come around again. Gregg Levoy has his own account of the ripple effect created by a recurring omen in his life. During a period when he did not know what he wanted from life and was wondering what to do next, he drove home from work one day and was listening on the radio to a song by the Eagles called "Desperado." As he pulled up to the curb in front of his house, he heard the last line of the song, which referred to the queen of hearts. Then, as he opened the door and stepped out of the car, a playing card appeared next to his left foot. It was the queen of hearts. After that, he found five more queen playing cards, all in highly improbable locations—such as a sand dune in Oregon and a mountain wilderness in Colorado, six miles from the nearest trailhead—absolutely beyond anyone's contriving.

Eventually Levoy became convinced that something profound was happening—that these phenomena were not occurring capriciously or without reason, but were promptings from a higher reality directing him toward using more heart in his life and his writing, and to inflect them both with the voice of the feminine—the queen being the archetype of powerful femininity.

In my own case, the unexpected appearance of the red shoes in the restaurant had also felt like a perfectly timed, precise sign of positive reinforcement and encouragement from the gods. Certainly it had plunged me into an immediate sense of optimism and fanned the flames of hope once again. But hope is a fragile affair that needs to be strengthened by success, and as far as I could tell, I wasn't having any. Even spring brought no real change in my situation.

I'm standing in front of the altar, yelling at the Black Madonna. "It's impossible," I state out loud. "We put this thing together, but it isn't working out. You must see that it isn't working!" I realize I've vowed to stick with this no matter what, but I'm back in yet another cycle of staving off despair. I'm back in that maddening shadowland of not wanting to go on.

After this little firing-squad performance, my body feels better. I gather up some books and papers and head out for the porch.

A few minutes later, I notice the white FedEx truck lumbering up the hill. Since I'm not expecting anything, I'm surprised when it pulls into my driveway, and the driver jumps out with a package. I ask him where it's from.

"Sam Gilliam, Washington, D.C.," he reads from the label.

I assume it contains a catalogue. Sam Gilliam is an African-American artist, well-respected in the Washington, D.C. art community. He is best known for his draped canvases, existing in unorthodox formats somewhere between painting and sculpture.

Sam and I met for the first time three or four months ago. I was giving a lecture at Radford University near Blacksburg, in the same week that Sam was doing a visiting-artist stint, spending a week hanging out with students in the art department. Sam came to my talk. We met afterwards at the reception, and I found him to be a dignified and strikingly attractive older man with a compendious interest in everything around him. He exuded a radiant warmth. In conversation, Sam expressed an interest in my Black Madonna altar. The following day, brought by the department chair and a couple of students, he came to see it.

We communed, in a nuanced way, over favorite objects on the altar, including the serendipitous red shoes from Kroger's. Then we all huddled amiably over tea and cookies, chatting and telling stories for several hours. Sam was enchanting. As they were getting ready to leave, I gave him one of my black mammy dolls to give to his daughter, who collects them. I will always remember the sweet way he posed, very solemnly for just a moment, in his raincoat, with the mammy doll festooned on his crescent arm, so his friends could enjoy the picture. And that was the last I had seen or heard from Sam.

It's quite common for artists to send me catalogues or announcements of shows; in a word, that's usually what they have on their minds. So I can't quite work out what's happening when, instead of a catalogue, a small box spills out of the cardboard FedEx envelope. The box has a label on the lid from a gift store in Ann Arbor, with a note stuck on top of it from the proprietor to Sam, stating that she very much hopes his friend will enjoy the present.

With great curiosity, I open the box. Inside is a pin—a small, eight-pointed gold sun, with a little convex plastic dome in its center that has a tiny photograph inside. At first I don't really understand. Why would Sam be sending me this odd piece of jewelry three months after we met? In mild confusion, I rotate the object around a bit in my hand, trying to decipher the red image under the plastic dome. Bewilderment turns to an eerie thrill as soon as I recognize the image. It's the red shoes.

"Each time I found another queen card," Levoy writes, " the sheer unthinkability of the occurrence took another giant step forward, and eventually the synchronicities went so far beyond the laws of probability that I can only barely hesitate to say it's *impossible* that there was nothing more going on than blind chance or dumb luck. Such an adroit arrangement of events and timing—such stagecraft—seemed orchestrated by something with wits."

Certainly encountering the same symbol more than once at pivotal moments of discouragement, and in unlikely circumstances, attracts the attention. But underneath my excitement there was a troubled confusion which nettled me at regular intervals. Was I really discovering a magical path, or was I just making it all up?

The physicist David Bohm has argued that matter, mind, and energy are mutually interactive, so that an intensely framed question has the power to call its answer from an ungraspable source of being that he calls the "implicate order." I don't really understand it, but I keep trying to assimilate this new thing, which seems to be a feature of my life now.

Sometime later, I ask the thesaurus: "Is this still my path?" "Bring to fruition, use, develop, make the most of."

So much of the time it feels like I'm sinking into quicksand, spinning my wheels. "How should I proceed?" "Aim high, refuse to give up hope, come up smiling, avoid defeat." It's as if I'm holding hands in the dark with some kind of exotic spiritual cheerleader.

"What is the best thing I can do, then?" "Hold the faith, right-minded, sound, balanced, assenting, undivided, unswerving, undeviating, loyal."

I'm not taking anything for granted. Since I'm interviewing who knows who or who knows what, as if I'd gone slightly mad, I have one last, crazy question. "Will I be protected?"

Like bell buoys sounding in the night, the answer comes back at me. I'm staring at these brazened, buttered words: "Adventure story, love story."

Twenty-six

I GO TO campus expecting to hear a routine lecture, but as soon as I scan the horizon, I can see I am about to attend some kind of monumental event. The turnout is dazzling; already there are people stacked up in the aisles. The speaker is Jane Goodall, the renowned primatologist and sophisticated savior of wild chimpanzees on the brink of extinction in Africa. To my amazement and delight, she turns out to have the humor of Woody Allen and the compassion of Kuan Yin.

There's only a 5% difference in DNA, she tells us right off the bat, between ourselves and the chimps. Cresting genially on this crisp statistic, she never once uses her touching respect for these compromised creatures as a foil to expose human shortcomings. Goodall is remarkably unstrident or tough-talking. Here is someone, I soon realize, who has passed through the eye of the patriarchal needle and come out the other side wondrously free of judgment. Driven by a quintessential openness of heart and innocence of spirit, she doesn't demonize the human perpetrators of species and habitat destruction because—and this is really significant, I think—she has found another voice that is not hostile or scornful. Goodall's answer to the excesses of patriarchy is to stand as a harbinger of hope—calm, composed, benevolent, and gentle as a lamb, no matter what is happening. And in her presence, others receive a taste, an aroma, of their own spiritual possibilities.

What does it mean to speak in a voice that is free of scorn? A voice that doesn't demonize? That doesn't patronize? Buddhists refer to this as "right speech." If you cannot say something in a way that others can appreciate hearing, then it is better to keep quiet.

This has been really brought home to me as a result of

synchronistically reading the blistering, angry comments of Mary Daly, "the *grande dame* of feminist theology," in an obscure magazine I found called *What Is Enlightenment?* Starting with the unlikely proposition that men should be demolished ("I don't think about men. I really don't care about them"), Daly's voice, inherently attacking, comes at you with a monkey wrench. Daly has taught at Boston College since 1974. Men are never allowed to attend her classes.

"I know how they think and I abhor it . . . I hate the 'human species'. . . . I hate what it is doing to this earth: the invasion of everything. . . . It's a totally invasive mentality—rapist."

Right or wrong, unfortunately her voice sabotages the message. Whereas Goodall's voice really affected me with its soft, flickering radiance—the absence of snap judgments or disdain was like breathing in honeysuckle—Daly's voice has the distinctive characteristics of patriarchy stamped all over it. Her oppressive lack of compassion sours the tone of liberation.

Of course she was one of the first to open up the whole can of worms and find something badly amiss. ("We're living in the hell of phallocracy, penocracy, jockocracy, cockocracy, call it whatever—patriarchy.") But that sustained look, at some deep level, seems to have turned her heart to stone and trapped her, consciously or unconsciously, in the same reflexive attitudes and behavior she condemns.

Daly, naturally, wouldn't agree with that. She wouldn't care. But the uncaring is what seems to me so alarmingly patriarchal. Every worldview has its pathological expression. "To surrender a worldview," as Ken Wilber points out in his journals, *One Taste*, "is a psychological earthquake somewhere around 7.0 on the internal Richter scale, and most people avoid this at all costs."

My old friend Ellen Dissanayake, who now lives in Seattle, informs me that she recently bought herself a 1920s upright Baldwin piano. Ellen and I have been friends ever since the 1970s when

TWENTY-SIX

she first turned up on my doorstep in London as a fellow author of books about the meaning and purpose of art. Ellen's perspective is scholarly and ethnobiological. She believes that art fulfills an evolutionary need of "making special" in the human species. It is a natural biological behavior that helps to bind human communities and societies together—a purpose that we both believe has been sadly defeated by art's conversion into an exercise of commodification in Western consumer society. Ellen's book, *Homo Aestheticus*, put her on the lecture circuit after it was published in 1992. Since then, she has traveled extensively, giving talks and attending conferences, and generally enjoying the academic outreach that is part of the scholar's business. I am quite startled, therefore, when she announces that her desire to continue along this road has reached its climax—and that an altogether new object of passion has crept up from behind.

"I suspect that the piano will put the last nail in the coffin of what I've been realizing is the dying of my scholarly, academic persona," she writes in her letter. "Perhaps it's too early to diagnose such a surprising possibility, but if I look in my deeper currents I can detect an increasing unwillingness to 'keep up' with the 'literature,' enter into the debates, worry about convincing the unpersuadable, write stuff for conferences, and so forth." As I read, I find myself nodding inwardly—another case of sliding identities.

"It just seems more and more that three books are enough, and now my message is out there and doesn't need me anymore to advance it." At this point I'm actually smiling. Without her even realizing it, Ellen's comments say everything to me about my own life—although her fidelity to footnotes has long outlived my own.

Many people, particularly women, seem to be rowing off the edge of old beliefs and letting them transform into something else. It used to be that "dropping out" referred to people who never finished high school. Then in the 1960s, hippies and Beats defected in droves from corporate America and the consumer life style. But now, our culture is running into yet another pandemic form of dropping out, which is neither social nor economic, but religious. The radical revolt against institutional religion and its patriarchal forms of power is the subject of a new book, sent to me for review by the Institute of Noetic Sciences in California. In *A Woman's Journey to God*, Joan Borysenko asks, "What are they dropping out from?" The obvious, if clunky, answer is: "God as a jealous, punitive white Anglo-Saxon male with a long beard." And if Borysenko is correct, we are just getting into the full swing of it.

I'm excited when I poke my nose into her book, because it seems to fit in perfectly with particular aspects of what I'm writing about myself. Consider the recent rash of women everywhere who are sharing their stories "over breakfast, in pajamas, in the bathroom, out on walks." Rather than seeking God from the outside in (the old religious model), they are seeking God from the inside out. Women are exploring their own spirituality and the feminine face of God. Many factors underlie this change, and few are better positioned to understand them than is Borysenko, who for many years has been conducting spiritual retreats and goddess gatherings. For many religious dropouts, she proclaims, these women's gatherings have become "church."

Women's spirituality, Borysenko explains, isn't lofty or remote. It "doesn't require scaling mountains, slaying dragons, or living in caves while dining on meager rations of locusts and wild honey." In the emergent feminine vision, we are simply part of things, "no more or less important that a tree, or a dog, or a river." Much of Borysenko's book is about the right to worship in our own way, using any form or image, without repression or persecution. In the 1960s women burned their bras. "Are we to burn our Bibles in the new millennium?" Borysenko asks.

Certainly I share the author's sense of the bankruptcy of organized religion. Still, my response to her book—which is welded together with improvisational spirituality of every sort, and is decisively eclectic—surprises me. In the new spirituality, the old gods are no longer absolute—there is more than one way to skin a cat. Borysenko herself is a naked example of this acculturation process—she is a Jew who loves Catholic churches, candles, holy water, and the Virgin Mary. She is also married to a Native American and leads pilgrimages to Sai Baba's ashram in Puttaparthi, India. "I was tempted to buy pictures of Baba to bring home," she writes at one point, "but could not figure out why I would want them. I already had a drawer overflowing with pictures of holy people." Besides, since every woman is herself a priestess, there is no need for the intercession of priests, ministers, or rabbis.

I suppose where my ambivalence enters is at Borysenko's mystic euphoria regarding the consolidation of women, secretly and essentially intertwined, and ready to burst into song at the slightest provocation. Towards the end of the book, she describes standing in line at a bank in Jerusalem, and finding herself next to an Arab woman dressed in a black chador, with whom she cannot speak because of the language barrier. Slowly, she becomes aware that she is having an experience of deep communion. "Our wombs were in silent communication." Then she realizes that "We could pray together, this Arab woman and I. We could work together for peace."

Personally I suppose I'm a little embarrassed by the womb-to-womb confabulation. Borysenko doesn't have much to say about spiritual life which begins at the end of one's comfort zone, or initiatic ordeals. "Women are relational stars," she writes. "We love company and conversation." Books can act as triggers, and this one prompts me to say something that is probably heretical, but I'll say it anyway: my own sense of spirituality requires from the seeker a peculiar internal state which ordinary life does not normally induce—a certain living on the edge. What would Borysenko think of this, I wonder, as a multilayered calesthenics for the self? As a firsthand experience of deep embodied communion?

In an extraordinary performance work called *Dragon Heads*, Marina Abramovíc sits for an hour inside a ring of ice, together with five pythons that writhe across her face and tangle themselves in her hair. It's a state of affairs requiring utter surrender and passivity in the face of danger, as the merest flicker of fear would trigger the snake's biting and strangling instincts.

If I seem to have overdrawn my picture here, it's because right at the moment, I can't stop thinking about this image. It stands out for me because of its dangerous edge. And reveals what I take to be the true face of spiritual inclusiveness: the dance of power between masculine and feminine energies, integrated and fused in symbiotic perfection. Without this synthesis, without this edge, we're still in the Rainbow Room, wearing ruby slippers.

My friend Michael Grosso says he has made a painting of Sai Baba and, in a solemn-playful mood, invited Baba to materialize his sacred ash *(vibhuti)* on the painting. Sai Baba is famous for his miraculous manifestations: rings, huge necklaces, and on occasion, steaming hot food, out of thin air. These miracles are his calling card; they get people's attention and inspire faith. Nothing's happened yet, but, Michael says, he'll keep me posted.

Twenty-seven

"LIFE," according to the lugubrious view of William Butler Yeats, "is a preparation for something that never happens." With its unrewarding message whispered into the thin air, Yeats's comment does not win my heart or put me in a festive mood. What if this is what's really going on?

This quest of mine is refusing to be led in the direction I set myself. Sometimes I try to concentrate on the story I would love to write, the one with the fairy-tale ending in which the girl falls to earth in a dead faint and suddenly the menacing demon stands before her as a beautiful man, robed in animal skins, whose secret intention all along has been to bring her to his white tent and make her happy. In fairy tales, only the one who completes all the tasks, who carries on until the dragon is slayed, wins the princess. Only the one whose will has been tempered and made strong by the struggle to overcome opposition and difficulty, and whose spirit has not been broken, succeeds.

"Human beings often strive for impossible things," Harry Moody and David Carroll write in *The Five Stages of Soul*, "spend their lives in vain pursuits, then discover too late that they have sought illusionary goals and wasted their precious years in a wrong kind of struggle." But how do you know when something is a wrong kind of struggle? You wait in vain, you are patient, hold on, bide time, to no avail, without success, achieve nothing. You are the only one stupid enough to be sleeping out in the winter storm, with a pool of water at your feet. You become an all too obvious study in futility. How do you know that a road is a dead end, unless you've gone all the way to the end of it?

"If a pursuit does not strike oil," writes Gregg Levoy, "it doesn't mean your effort lacked value or integrity. Perhaps you were meant to try something and find it *not* to your liking, so that you could cross it off your list once and for all." That's one way to look at things. But does it really fit with anyone's idea of a successful outcome?

"I'm standing at the window, and I ask myself why the miracle I'm waiting so desperately for doesn't happen. And I ask myself: Did I choose the wrong path?"

I didn't write this, though I certainly could have. The question is posed by Brazilian author Paulo Coelho, as he looks soberly out of the window in a motel room in the Mojave Desert. The writer has come to this place on a real-life metaphysical quest—a provocative adventure that he describes in his book *The Valkyries*. He has risked everything on a bet that his guardian angel would show itself within forty days and speak to him in this place. On the thirty-eighth day, Coelho has still seen nothing and is afraid of the bitter lesson he may be about to learn: the lesson of disappointment.

"It will happen or it won't. Let's not waste our energy discussing it," he says to his wife, before setting out one last time into the desert, alone.

Later that day, he nearly passes out from fright when a voice instructs him to kneel down and clear the ground, after which a golden arm appears and begins to write his name in the sand.

Coelho got his miracle. Will I ever get mine? So far, whenever I find myself on pins and needles, needing deeper insights into life and cosmos, I have usually called on the special assistance of a psychic friend of mine. Tom Williams is a musician, living in a nearby town, who aspires to great fluency in the psychic realms. He is able to catch, understand, and interpret images in a very compelling way. His visionary readings for me over the past few years are by now one of my favorite routines. A benevolent cosmic eavesdropper, he arrives today to assess the situation with his special deck of cards and his photosensitive sixth sense.

TWENTY-SEVEN

After tuning in, Tom presents me with an unexpected and idiosyncratic little scenario that is quite disturbing. He sees my Tom laid out on a baking pan and rolled into a large oven—where he cooks like dough and then emerges in the form of a chicken. The chicken has a lid on it, which can be taken off. Inside is a plate with a piece of paper that has something written on it. Tom asks if I would like him to read what it says. I nod for him to proceed. Then, as if finding the inscription of an indelible watermark, he pronounces these words: "I'm chicken-hearted."

For a few seconds, I can't move a muscle or a cell. The deadly precision disorients me. My whole world suddenly turns inside out from this primitive whack of truth. Not that I wasn't aware that a relationship was something that would strain Tom's every nerve and shake up his belief patterns. I already knew that. But I still harbored the impression that this was no ordinary man, and if anyone could, he would unobtrusively triumph over any impediments based on fear. The warrior's code of honor was not exactly geared to avoidance or flight. There is only one position, for the warrior, in which to face the battle of life: frontally. The warrior never withdraws. He is identified, in his idea of the self, with courage. These were moral facts for anyone who was cultivating his (or her) "dragon nature."

Closely entwined with the fearless man of courage, however, and forcing conflict on it, was the archetypal chicken-heart. Although they seemed to contradict each other, I could see that each was correct in a certain way, and that both were simultaneously true. The association was intimate and necessary. One only arrived at fearlessness by transforming one's fear. The question was, would one of them win out eventually? The tension of such a dialectic could be highly unpredictable.

The *I Ching* warns me not to interfere. "The powers of the status quo are formidable," it says, "and not to be tampered with. Quell any impulse to take aggressive measures. Your choice is either to acquiesce and wait out the restrained atmosphere in a friendly manner, or to depart from the relationship altogether. Do not attempt to influence others, for this is not possible. There is nothing you can do."

My psychic friend proposes waiting until the end of October for events to clarify, which is still several months away. Then he suggests that I will be released from my inner vow to stick with the situation no matter what, and can remove myself, if that is what I want, from the whole unsettling tangle of wires.

"Each moment the true warrior must cut through her story, and step forth from her vision," Thomas Crum states in *Journey to Center*. At this point, all I can do is follow the course of events and go wherever they might take me. It all boils down to one thing: this is my life. I am not making any of it up, and I will not get to choose how it ends. Because, as don Juan tells Carlos Castaneda, "infinity chooses. The warrior-traveler simply acquiesces in the choice." I realize that my desire to succeed is trapping me, and that I will have to let go of it. Psyche's faith is her willingness to submit to the inevitable. She simply incubates the situation and waits for events to clarify.

So what is wanted of me now? I've flung today's question at the Thesaurus like an old tennis ball. "Ethos, habitual character, moral significance, behave well, carry on, be master of one's own ship."

The notion that possible futures can exist in a kind of suspended or limbo state—until just one of them is actually selected by our observation—is an old one in quantum physics. It was demonstrated by Erwin Schrödinger, who created a thought-only exercise in 1935 famously known as "Schrödinger's box," in which a cat is put in an enclosed chamber with radioactive material and a monitoring device. Until the box is opened, there is a fifty percent chance the cat will be dead, and a fifty percent chance it will be alive. Both possibilities exist side by side until the moment when an observer opens the box and looks in.

I decide that Schrödinger's box may be an artful equivalent for holding the tensions in my own situation—until infinity wins through and makes its choice. To construct my own version, I will not need much. From the altar, I select a round, smooth, gray stone about an inch in diameter to stand for the man of courage—endowed with the energy of completion, fulfillment, success. Then I pick out a small, thin crystal. It will represent the chicken-heart—the opportunity not taken, the missed connection.

Placing both objects side by side into a small cardboard box, I slowly bind up the box, mummylike, with a long ribbon of white eyelet and place my new sacred totem back on the altar. Until the box is opened, all the possibilities—success and failure, yes and no, chicken-heart and man of courage—coexist together, but once the box is opened, one of the options becomes reality and the other disappears.

So much for the container of things. I have no real idea of why I'm doing this, but somehow reducing my problem to the dimensions of an abstract geometry creates a kind of force field that can act on the passing of time, until it is ready to display its results.

Twenty-eight

LIKE A METEOR hitting the ground, Julia Butterfly Hill has come down after living for two years one hundred and eighty feet in the air, on a four-by-seven wooden platform, strapped to the branch of a thousand-year-old redwood tree and covered with a tarpaulin.

Julia Butterfly took up residence in the California redwood in December 1997, as part of a tree-sit organized by the radical environmental group Earth First! to save the tree from clearcutting. When no one else volunteered to replace her, she stayed on, living without heat, bath, toilet, electricity, safety, or certainty she'd ever come down. Pacific Lumber did its best to scare her out of the tree, blowing air sirens all night long, shining floodlights, and shouting threats and insults. Enraged loggers felled trees in her direction, and when all else had failed, company security guards tried to starve her out with a ten-day blockade at the foot of the tree. Sometimes the cold turned her feet black. At times she came close to dying, blasted by ninety mile-an-hour winds, battered by icy rain and snow. In more settled moments, she spent her time in the tree talking to politicians, radio stations, and journalists on her battery-powered cell phone.

Just after midnight on December 11, 1999, Julia Butterfly was able to come down, when a deal was negotiated with the timber company, who agreed to sell the tree and three acres of the surrounding forest to her for $50,000—using money raised by her supporters in twenty-four hours.

The spiritual force of this experience elicits awe—an inner resolve so amazing and fierce it penetrates to the core and pierces right through. The level of commitment instructs. It illuminates one's perspective on everything.

At some point we all raid the world to find a symbol of what life means to us. Recognizing that I have found mine—a twenty-five-year-old woman who has lived into, and then surpassed, her own limits and remained true to her quest—I tear out a photograph from *Elle* magazine of her iridescent face, frame it, and put it on the altar. The tender sweetness of her gaze defies description; it's a bit like being wrapped in scented tissue.

How can I find this depth of truth and commitment in my own life? "The ultimate question, the one I can't answer, is: How do you come up with a soul that's willing to go all the way?" Ever since I first happened on this question, posed by my friend Stephanie Mills, an environmental writer, in one of her books, I have felt challenged. And I have learned something about myself, about how I am and how I would like to be. I want to become a soul who is willing to go all the way.

Each of us, it seems, constructs a world from the fragments of information, and the insights, at our disposal. Destinies are never finished outcomes, given once and for all—they only disclose themselves as fragments. But we are held back or pushed forward by the construction of reality we create with our stories.

"Who are we," asks Italo Calvino at the end of *Six Memos for the Millenium*, ". . . if not a combinatoria of experiences, information, books we have read, things imagined? Each life is an encyclopedia, a library, an inventory of objects, a series of styles, and everything can be constantly shuffled and reordered in every way conceivable."

Everything is collage. In a sense, the parts "give themselves." Living the magical life means learning to recognize and connect them to the whole. We are translators and mediators in the field from which our experience arises. In this field, all is analogy, relation, revelation, by the laws of correspondence. Imagination is

TWENTY-EIGHT

what opens the connection between one level and another.

I have a dream in which I am riding in my friend Susan's car. We are inside of a garage. Backing up, it feels like the car is going to crash into a wall. Panicked, I look down and notice that there is no steering wheel. "Don't worry," Susan says. "The car knows where to go and it will take us there. Just lean back and relax. You'll see, you'll love it." As she says this, the car goes into reverse and heads, easily and flawlessly, out of the garage.

The message may not be clear to anyone else, but it is clear to me. I understand its meaning as if it were speech: the universe is a better organizer than you could ever think of being, so give it a chance and stay out of the way. Surrender to the world, receive it in your stillness

> And it will happen. For miracles gravitating
> To earth, know just where people will be waiting.
> And eagerly will find the right address
> And tenant, even in a wilderness. (Joseph Brodsky)

I have just returned from visiting friends in Boone, North Carolina and seeing an exhibition of Day of the Dead altars at Appalachian State University. It is five o'clock in the afternoon on the last day of October and the sky is stained with pink as the sun begins to lower. Halloween. My day of reckoning, according to what Tom Williams said. What happens when you are at your lowest point and you can no longer imagine pulling victory out of the jaws of defeat?

No angel of deliverance has come, but a new mood of acceptance has taken over. The mental churning has ceased. I'm no longer waiting for anything, pursuing anything, anticipating anything. I have long feared this moment, but now that it is finally here, my mind has loosened its grip.

I look at the eyelet-covered reminder of my attempt at metaphysics in a match-box that still sits on the altar. Hammered out in a moment of tremendous odds, the whole stratagem feels redundant now, a pointless effort towards puzzling out possibilities of "this" or "that." I need to unbundle the box, dismantle its contents. At this point, there is nothing to "know," nothing else to do. There is no more basis for going on.

But first I decide to open the mail. Something is sticking out at the bottom of the small pile. A quick examination reveals yet another FedEx parcel from Sam Gilliam. And then a bracelet falls out and I see the flash of red shoes, each pair glowing under a tiny Plexiglas dome, attached at intervals like buttons to a gold link chain.

I put on the bracelet and take a deep breath. What is the probability of something like this happening by chance—three times in succession? I would have to agree with the Apache shaman, Ernesto Alvarado, who holds that if something recurs three times, then we need to give it our attention and respect. Alvarado states, in Timothy Freke's book *Shamanic Wisdomkeepers*, "Ask yourself once a month: 'Am I where I'm supposed to be? Am I doing what I'm supposed to be doing?' . . . And then begin to look for things that are beyond coincidence. I would say it should happen three times. Then you think: 'Maybe I'd better listen because those spirit guys are trying to contact me.'" There seemed to be some kind of aesthetic perfection in the way the invisible world was slipping me clues and holding this chain of events together through the medium of the red shoes, magically weaving my story. I had experienced enough instances of this to be finally convinced.

A few minutes later, I proceed to disassemble the matchbox, peeling back the layers of white eyelet. Slowly I open it up, at which point I have a perception as powerful and startling as a loud knock on the door. I find myself staring down at only a single object—the gray stone. At first I don't believe what I see—my mind resists this commanding detail—but contrary to all reasonable expectations it appears that the crystal, symbolizing the chicken-heart, has disappeared. The realization starts slowly, then picks up speed as my consciousness suddenly registers this thought: once the box is opened, and we look inside it, one of the options becomes reality and the other disappears. This is the fundamental principle of Schrödinger's box. But I had never expected it to actually "work."

Only after further exploration, poking around in the box, do I discover the crystal, buried beneath the small wad of cotton. But the discovery fails to break the spell of whatever it is that has just happened, and the special force attached to the magic way the stone has shown itself, like the pole of a magnetic field, at just the right moment in my story. Nothing in the real world has changed, but once again I have been shot through with a sense of excitement. It's as if, like a long distance runner who no longer feels any pain, my mind has entered "the zone."

I want my body to receive this impress, like a mandatory seal, not to be trifled with. Psyche's secret has finally become transparent to me: Let go of the consciousness of disappointment. Release your belief in the promise unfulfilled. Sacrifice the need to know, and trust the invisible processes that are at work. Develop a mind that can work with whatever happens. Allow everything to be all right as it is and simply remain true to the quest. When you learn to stop struggling and do nothing, everything is possible. Submit, surrender, become an embodiment of the feminine principle. Don't assume you know the right answer in advance. We are simply part of the vaster design that is unfolding.

In the world itself this is, of course, exactly what we are so reluctant to do. Our whole culture has gone in a contrary direction. "You are not staying in suspense," writes David Richo in *Unexpected Miracles*, "because it works, but because that is the only thing you can do." This is what trust is like—the creative principle operating out of the deep feminine. Most of us don't let ourselves believe something can happen unless we see ahead of time how all the pieces are going to fit together.

Italo Calvino ends his second Memo, the one on "Quickness," with a wonderful Chinese story. "Among Chuang-tzu's many skills, he was an expert draftsman. The king asked him to draw a crab. Chuang-tzu replied that he needed five years, a country house, and twelve servants. Five years later the drawing was still not begun. 'I need another five years,' said Chuang-tzu. The king granted them. At the end of these ten years, Chuang-tzu took up his brush and, in an instant, with a single stroke, he drew a crab, the most perfect crab ever seen."

If equivalence is truly the rule—if everything really is analogy, relation, or revelation—then the crab is a matter of some significance to the end of my story, a signal winging in at me from the cosmos to settle back a little deeper into the saddle. "All I had to do was to follow my inner promptings," wrote Hermann Hesse. "Why was it so difficult?"

By now it has become dark outside. I vault over to my oracle. "Will it mean a happy ending, success story, victory, triumph?" I unloose the question for the last time to those irascible deities that control the dictionary. "Paradox: that which is contrary to received opinion; that which is apparently absurd but is or may be really true." I had to smile. The dictionary always surprises me with its strong and original prose. Sinking down into my chair, I shoot a last query to the thesaurus: "Will Eros return?" The rogue answer rumbles out: "Unexpected, without warning, unannounced, not expect or look for, think unlikely, come up from behind, appear from nowhere."

Twenty-nine

SNAKES are one of the great mythological creatures of the world, associated with renewal, change, and the casting off of old skins. But I definitely wasn't thinking about any of this on that Sunday morning when the small black head suddenly protruded through a hair space between the cabinet under the kitchen sink and the narrow wedge of wood paneling supporting it from the floor. I'd been cutting up tomatoes—friends were coming to lunch—when I noticed something that looked like a short piece of black strap lying limply on the floor.

At least, I told myself it had to be a strap, even though I knew the only things inside the cabinet were a pair of yellow rubber gloves, a plunger, and a bunch of old plastic shopping bags. Later on I would watch, aghast, as the "strap" finally dragged its ominous length slowly across the kitchen floor. End to end, the snake was almost five feet long.

By that time, my friend Betty had come to the rescue in response to my emergency phone call. She wasn't afraid of snakes, she said, and once the snake was fully out in the room, she tried to immobilize it with a floor mop and grab it by the tail. But the snake got away from her and, flattening itself, it retreated back through the same hairline crack, only this time, now facing in the opposite direction, it disappeared directly underneath the stove. Absolutely terrified, I did the only thing I could think of: I turned on the oven. The snake did not reappear, but it had unleashed a terrible irrational fear in me—a primal fear. I felt as if I could never live safely in my house again.

Then Betty left. The other lunch guests had not yet arrived. And during the time I was alone, I saw the snake leave, too. Was it a "coincidence" that I happened to look out of the kitchen window at the precise moment it was making its way through the grass? I probably would have assumed so, except for the message, which felt as if it were being delivered like a clear voice in my ear. The transmission was vivid and charged and unmistakable: "This is the snake. It's gone now, and you need to see that with your own eyes."

Only then did I begin to register that maybe this was another omen of some kind, though I had, in that moment, no idea of what it might mean.

Two days later, I had a telephone conversation with a friend whom I do not speak with all that often. I told him about the horrifying visit of the snake. He didn't respond the way most people did, by saying "Oh my God!" or "So how did you get rid of it?" Instead he asked me if I had figured out what the snake meant.

I told him that I'd been going over it in my mind, and had indeed come to suspect that the snake's appearance might have something to do with Tom, but that I didn't know what it was yet.

"That was my hit, too," he said, much to my surprise. "Maybe it's time to tell him about the book."

His words almost made my heart fall on the spot. As soon as I heard them, my instinctive self understood what the snake visitor was telling me. The snake in my kitchen had been only a practice run. The time had come to confront the archetypal snake in my life.

As I've made quite clear, I believe that oracles come from many places besides dreams and divination—they are streaming in steadily from the everyday world around us. Only minutes before my conversation, I'd stapled together some Xerox copies of an extract from my book, which had just been published in the *Noetic Sciences Review*, a quarterly magazine concerned with the frontiers of consciousness research, put out by the Institute of Noetic Sciences in California. The editors were intrigued by my story of placing the votive box in the stream and having it returned to me later. These were circumstances about which Tom knew nothing. Indeed, Tom had no idea his presence was so strategic in what I was writing at all.

Before the snake, before the telephone call, I'd had no thought of sending Tom the article. I saw what I was writing as an immense labor of love, but even so, my attraction to the story was always coupled with a legitimate fear of failure, so I had kept everything pretty much under wraps. Now I realized that one must speak one's part and do one's deed at that point in the drama where the play calls for it—so I sent him the article.

Two days later I received a phone call. Immediately I could feel the crackle of anger beneath the surface as Tom let me know that he was really upset by what I'd written. "There never was in the past, and there never will be in the future, any romantic relationship between us," he said, in a terse voice clearly intended to leave me no choice but to go along. What is more, he informed me, being represented in that light would reflect badly on the authority of his teaching reputation. Then he asked me to return his book.

"In the presence of the lady, in the space of the Grail mystery, the armor is to be shed, the weapons left behind," writes Edward C. Whitmont in *Return of the Goddess*. Only it wasn't going to happen. The patriarchal ego would hold tight—unapologetic, guiltless, and invulnerable. In that moment it was as if a great iron gate had just swing shut, and something snapped in me. A man who cared more for the image of his authority than for the truth of love was not someone I could go down the same road with anymore.

I could feel myself take a deep breath as I let this unexpected possibility shatter any existing state of hope. I thought again about the sentence that had crossed my path earlier that morning in a book I was reading, which now seemed to put its own intrinsic logic to work on my behalf: "He's afraid he won't live up to expectations, and he defends himself against these expectations, against his fear if failure, by striking out at you." Then I thought of the Apache warrior, Geronimo, photographed after he had been imprisoned for years at Fort Sill, Oklahoma, defiantly staring the camera down and making it clear that whatever had been taken from him, he had given up nothing.

But this time, I don't let myself go there. I need to be done with filling my notebook with such exercises. Let Tom's disclaimer stand for the record. He has spoken his part. It has just as much "truth" in it as any thought or feeling of mine.

On the phone, I didn't challenge his statement, but answered as simply as I could. "You know, you could have said what you just said to me at any time. But you never did."

A few days later, I wake up in the middle of the night and realize that I am having a Rosa Parks moment. In everybody's life, there is that moment when a true moral self has to step forward and defend its own truth, whatever comes of it.

It is possible that my image of Tom has been bigger and more possibility-laden than the person; and if that is really the case, then I may just have found myself, by some strange combination of imagination and inspiration, in the somewhat odd position of preferring a picture of reality over the reality itself. But I have no intention of dismissing my reality as wrong—or as "nothing but" a fantasy. I have lived this story with my whole being and have earned my own version of the tale. Nor do I feel the necessity of being pinned down by a single immovable interpretation of what has happened. "The mythographer knows what the therapist knows," writes James Hollis, "that there is no one truth, that all the variants, even contradictory ones, are somehow true."

During the weeks preceding and just after the snake's visit, the divining process remained a prophetic constant, straightening out areas of psychic entanglement, preparing me for what was to come. It told me to watch for refusals, nonacceptance, being turned down—that a stifling relationship was about to end. It told me to accept the inevitable and to handle loss with grace. Not to throw myself away where there was no receptivity. The guidance I received told me to embrace things not working out. Psychic death would prove to be a blessing in disguise and would clear the way for something better.

TWENTY-NINE

It seems that I have finally reached that part in the myth in which there is a bottoming out of all presuppositions in order to become utterly receptive—that part where, in a posture of vulnerability and cosmic surrender, Psyche falls into a swoon. Psyche passes her final initiation by demonstrating trust in her own inner authority above all other authority. Everything must be attempted without the promise of consummation. She waits without hope.

After the phone call, my fate seemed like it was sealed. But today at lunch, my Chinese fortune cookie says "You must extract yourself from a dilemma by making a choice." It sounds a bit ominous, as I'm not sure what choices are left to me now. And then I remember my snake dream.

I am walking to my car when I discover that there is a large jungle snake coiled up underneath it. I'm afraid to open the door and step into the car. Wondering what to do, I accost a man who is passing by and ask him whether he thinks it would be safe to open the door. "Absolutely not!" he replies. "No way." Just then, another man appears. He notices the snake, goes straight over to the car, bends down and picks it up. I watch as he cradles the snake in his arms and croons to it in a loving way. Dumbfounded, I jump into the car and drive off—only to discover that the brakes aren't working.

Like driving, love is a skill you learn by doing. Immediately I recognize myself in the reaction of the first man. It's the same energy that infused my response to Tom's defiant rebuff. An iron gate swings shut and you don't make another approach. You don't even keep the door ajar.

I realize what my choice is. Without any confirmation from the "outside" world, can I still make the desperate gamble of trusting myself and others? Should I assume that my mystical experiences have all been false, or should I stand behind what my heart tells me? Can I "invest in loss"?

In that moment, the girl recognizes that the realization of her fate lies in accepting the spirit who persecuted her. She is able to put aside old disappointments and regrets, and boldly steps forward as the self she has wanted to be. That self is the second man in my dream. The fear, always an obstacle to enlightenment, is gone.

"We pass through cruel ordeals on the way," my friend M. C. Richards once wrote. " By going through the experience faithfully we may come through on the other side of the crossing point and find that our faithfulness has borne a new quality into the world."

The choice, then, is to speak freely in my own voice and allow my own personal truth to emerge. With new energy and passion, I can now embrace all the unseen forces that move to guide, inspire, and assist me. This spiritual realization has become more real to me than any outside experience of the world.

Like Psyche, I have emerged from this Dante-esque journey with my feminine soul intact. Something has carried me through to a safe ground. I no longer feel alone. And who knows what other gifts may yet rise phoenix-like out of the burnt-out ashes of this experience? From now on, deep down in my being, at whatever the cost, I intend to take seriously the rigors and splendors of living the magical life. Never again will I reduce life to just the ordinary and the mundane. Or hold on to anything as though it's the final story.

Epilogue

SOMETIMES it is not given to us to understand why things happen the way they do. The mystery is not lessened, however, because it cannot be explained. I realize I have written a book that is not only baffling in some ways, but is also subject to many possible distortions of subjective response. Committing myself to such a negative and apparently hopeless situation seems to throw out all the rules we have in place for such things. Psychological buttons get pushed; the story seems to drive people's psyches like a Rorschach, prompting others to offer their own versions of the meaning of these events off the page, as it were.

The fact that Tom ultimately refused to break out of his isolation and reciprocate my feelings is for some an occasion to wag their finger. They view my attachment to such an unsatisfying relationship as a glaring example of the "woman who loves too much"— who, abdicating good sense, leaves her roses in the vase long after they have withered.

Others will want to save me from the false hopes and the humiliation of a certain kind of mistake: the refusal to accept "reality." What they see is a flagrant case of inner perception not jibing with outer reality, making them wonder if the whole thing was not just a delusion, or a fantasy.

In C. S. Lewis's version of the Psyche myth, a novel called *Till We Have Faces*, Lewis builds his tale around the fact that Psyche lives in a palace that is "invisible" to everyone else. Orual, Psyche's stepsister (who, in Lewis's story really loves Psyche and has raised her from birth like a mother) goes to the mountain where Psyche has been left as a sacrifice to the gods to look for her bones so she can bring them back and bury them. But instead of bones, she finds Psyche, alive and well, prosperous and happily married to a god she has never seen. When Psyche invites Orual into her "palace," Orual doesn't see any palace and decides that Psyche must be mad.

"Psyche," she says to her step-sister, "this is sheer raving. You can't stay here. . . . There's no home here."

Psyche shakes her head, a little wearily. "It's no use, Maia," she said. "I see it and you don't. Who's to judge between us?" The next morning Orual has a brief glimpse of the palace rising up out of the fog, but decides that she must be hallucinating.

What bestows reality on our experience of life? In our outer-directed Western world, we talk about inner and outer as though they are diametrically opposed, and we act as though the physical world were the only "real" world. Only exteriors exist. A lot of people make the mistake of assuming that if other people haven't voted on it, something isn't real. In this context, my haunting bolero of love and loss seems to evade the common tests for reliability and validity almost entirely, since it infrequently meets any external object. The film maker Eric Rohmer once said to an interviewer, "What I call a *conte moral* is not a tale with a moral, but a story which deals less with what people do than with what is going on in their minds while they are doing it."

"Investing in loss"—a "subtle energy" practice in Chinese internal martial arts, where you absorb a blow by sinking and strengthening your root, so that nothing can knock you off base—is not the usual way we respond to negative circumstances in an outer-directed culture. Most people externalize conflict. They do not use inner alchemy to sustain the tension until the energies become balanced and unified. They do not work on life from the inside out. The fact that most of the experiences described here have occurred on the inner planes in no way diminishes their emotional and spiritual meaningfulness. Every bit of this felt real to me. You could say that in the process, my mind's own way of knowing has changed.

EPILOGUE

As a reader, you may enjoy this book in the light of the considerations I have just outlined. On the other hand, you may reject it for its unresolved dissonances and contradictions. But the story itself lacks nothing: its job is done.